TABULA RASA

What You Must Know About Success, Leadership, & Management

King Bless

KRBE

KNOWING RECEIVING BELIEVING THE ELITE

Detroit

Copyright © 2013 by KRBE LLC

For information about special discounts for bulk purchases, please contact king@kingbless.com
You can check out my site here: www.kingbless.com
Twitter: @kingblessdotcom
Facebook: @kingblessdotcom
Instagram: @kingblessdotcom

ISBN 978-0-9910705-0-3
Manufactured in the United States of America
FIRST EDITION
1 2 3 4 5 6 7 8 9 10

"If you are not ready to lead and succeed as much as you need air to breathe and live, then this book is not for you. You either don't know enough, don't care enough, or you're in fear of the status quo..."

CONTENTS

BOOK III
MANAGEMENT

BOOK IV
UNTITLED

I ask all my clients to read this guide in a serene environment. An environment that is conducive to learning and peace. Allow yourself this personal space to frequent during the reading of this guide as well as far after its completion. Here the atmosphere should emit an aura of positivity through smell, sight, touch, and sound. Amplify whatever those senses are that put you in your happy place. Positive immersion is critical while studying this guide, so upon the application of these methods you are cool and composed. Once you become engaged in tense environments, you will have a readily available memory and place which primary purpose is to refocus and calm your mind and prepare it for the task at hand. This is the outlet that will allow you to think clear in stressful situations.

Humans are born innate, however from the moment a person starts to experience life—see, feel, touch, hear, taste— assumptions are made and these become paradigms stored cognitively to allow quick instinctive access to similar thoughts. Do not worry about finding yourself because you are not you. You are what the world and environment shaped you to be. Merely a reaction of pre-determined patterns of behavior bottled up in a life form. Instead hit the reset button and go back to that innate stage. Tabula Rasa. Ready yourself to see the world in a new, prosperous, paradigm. Who you become should be better than who you are. Create yourself.

Look out for the keys to success.

Preface

There are several stories of people showing extraordinary strength and resilience in stressful times or when they were under extreme duress. Once a woman's baby was under a car and she reportedly lift the car to save her child. Or the Canadian mother standing toe-to-toe with a polar bear to rescue her endangered kids. Many people can even recount a time when they—or someone they knew—did an unbelievable act to prevail in a low-probability circumstance. What if you could tap into that reservoir of power at any time and you could keep it up at all times. The way you work in life, the things you do, and your accomplishments will all be extraordinary. This is the key that will lead to great prosperity.

In today's tough economic times, everyone is following the herd. Moving from place to place to find out where the next great job is or the most inexpensive way of living.

You should not want to settle for this mode of living. Reacting to every spin in the market is the same as being put on the ropes in boxing. Instead you should be enjoying a constant high quality life. Why should a person not be able to afford the luxuries life has to offer? Some people work hard and set their goals high and some don't. The ones who do should be rewarded deservingly. You must become the Sheppard, used as an agent to lead the herd, not follow. This agent is referred to as a SL (Successful Leader). Enlightened and sound, mentally and physically. Every day a SL is held to a higher standard to continuously display the characteristics and competence of what it takes to reach the elite.

SLs: work harder and are better under pressure, are good teammates, acclimate well to new surroundings, are dedicated, determined, and disciplined. SLs: can think on their feet, make important decisions in an instant, are accountable, responsible, thrive on competition, and are results oriented. They: have proven time-management skills, take instruction/ criticism, understand goal progression, are proven leaders, and can network with a variety of other SLs who all have the same traits. In addition SLs have an infinite amount of mental toughness and self-confidence. This group can overcome failure and disappointment, they are highly motivated and committed, possess concentration and focus, are optimistic and positive, strive to improve, teachable and love their work. Those who master the characteristics see a drastic change in their lives and attain the upmost pleasures; wealth, knowledge, health, culture and tranquility. Upon the completion of this transition, one will be able to win with any team, all doors will open to you, and you will have the ability to become the *business* for any market. Not becoming a SL can and will lead to economic failure, career ceilings, and misery in many aspects of your life.

An abundance of literature similar to this has been written giving the traits, habits, and definitions of success or leadership. While all these readings contain quality tips, majority of them give you the tips out of order or offer a lot of

[1]"fluff" to fill up pages. They are giving you a destination, but no clear path. These books metaphorically present a mountain to where you should be in life and give you the tools for climbing, but they don't show you how to use them or which way to go. In many of the books the pages are filled with "I"s. Things that the author did, or who they worked with (name dropping), or methods they used to get desired results. Occasionally these authors preach about leadership and humility, while often they simultaneously purge their pages with arrogance. Well if an Olympic swimmer decides to cross a river by swimming that may not be the best way for you. The swimmer can tell you hundreds of anecdotes as to how they developed, who has mentored them, and things they have accomplished—it still will not help. Maybe in your case a boat or jet ski is needed to cross that same river. This guide has the best methods for anyone to use. This guide, Tabula Rasa, will show you the [2]path to becoming a successful leader in a chronological order. This path is free from obstacle, straight to the point. The best of other readings, hints, tips, and tricks have already been integrated. Follow the signs on this path and you will find what you are looking for out of life and become one colossal step closer to attaining it. There is no inflated verbiage. You will transform into a SL.

---

[1] Filler, countless examples of personal experiences that add value to the author, not the material. Usually used to make the book longer or appear knowledgeable. Instead it dissipates precious time, which can be used to do something more significant.

[2] The path is just the metaphorical term for a model to prosperity, and without a good model to prosperity you will diminish.

The elite have reached the top of their realm and this inevitably puts them in a position of leadership. Whether it is expected or volunteered, often it subjects the holders of elite status to pressures to maintain that leadership position as a part of their newfound being. This is seen in famous athletes. Those who choose not to be "appropriate" role models are shunned by society for not accepting their role as a leader. Being a SL is more than just a title. It involves serious changes including lifestyle, attitude, and thought patterns. Instead of looking for a job, you look for a career. Not a career where you will be a subordinate your whole [1]life, but a career in which you are a boss, owner, or CEO. Why would you wake up and say I need to find someone to work for? More than likely the person or job you are applying to, already has a number two—vice president or manager, whatever the case may be. So in actuality you are waking up to say, how I can be a number three, four, or five, etc. today. If you were playing for a sports team, that is like going into a season saying how can we win sixth place this year. It is totally backward. Instead every day you should be honing your most precious resource, you. So that one day you can wake up and say how do I, how do we take over this new market, or even better create a market.

---

[1] There is nothing wrong with being a subordinate your whole life. Nothing is wrong with working for anyone else or just working a regular nine to five. However it is not for everyone. Elaborations will continue throughout guide.

Every part of this guide deals with failure; failure to be successful, failure to become a leader, and failure of managing your life. This is intentionally done so you can start to look at every aspect of your life as a lesson and begin to get the messages that have already been sent to you in some form or another. By dissecting experiences you begin to see what the chemical make-ups of them are. Some things you read in this guide you may have already been doing in your life, but you did not have a word or concrete formula for the method. You must know why you do things to elevate yourself and succeed at an elite level. Luckily, learning how is the easy part. By following this guide, you can also learn how to apply the methods without second thought. Once you begin to deliberately break down your experiences and understand the data driven way you think about things, you can begin to process and store that information cognitively. This is turn will give you a reformed "gut instinct" you can rely on in life.

This guide is separated into four books; Success, Leadership, Management and Untitled. For some, these books will serve as primers to their newfound posture; for others it will reinforce and enhance methods they already may use. Either way these books are magnificent in building a foundation, giving a blueprint, and providing insight as a finishing school.

Success and Leadership will reveal and impart how to derive the origins of a SL from within. Management will support the way you command and operate these robust capabilities. Untitled will be the book you write.

Tabula Rasa will make you take a journey inwards, inside of you. Here is where you will re-create and refine yourself.

King Bless

BOOK I

SUCCESS

Before a person is aware of any talents they possess a purpose for using them is presented. For example, someone would never know they are a fast runner if the opportunity for running never arose. Or a student would not know that they are good in math if they never had a reason to count anything or figure out an equation. The purpose for knowing this information must be fully analyzed to promote your direction in life. Before commencing examination of SL qualities you must acquire an understanding of your purpose, so that everything done from this point forward will be done with a passion. It will become a journey itself and it will inevitably lead you to whatever it is you genuinely want to pursue in life. This purpose is the destination to which the path you are now traveling will lead. Book I deals with concepts and the new paradigm for which you will see the world. Certainly the most important because here you get your passion then you incorporate the knowledge and direction it takes to become a SL.

Success is growing to reach your maximum potential, achieving your purpose in life, and attaining prosperity.

Chapter 1

WHAT IS YOUR SELF-WORTH

The average person will hear this question and think of how much they are due to make this year, how much money they can receive after liquidating their assets, and how much money is in their bank account. That is net worth. Some definitions of self-worth have been correlated to self-esteem, how you perceive or appraise yourself in a psychological manner. Neither of these statements are viable in a market to thrive in, in a pragmatic sense. Just because you already have money or you feel good about yourself does not mean you are successful or on your way to success. Reality television stars have money and many feel good about themselves, but by definition would they be considered a SL? Are any of these people the type you would obey, or better yet follow? And if so, would it be because of the dollar sign associated with the person or the actual person?

Self-worth is based around the total you. Self-worth is the totality of your knowledge, skills, and abilities, their viability in today's market, the realistic expectation of your growth overtime, and the difficulty of replacing you. The amount of rewards and positions you are offered or are capable of receiving for what you supply is directly proportionate to the demand.

You must know your own self-worth. As a sports metaphor, it's the players striking back. A prevalent example is how current NBA player LeBron James left what his team, the Cleveland Cavaliers, considered him as a sure bet, to the Miami Heat. Not only that, James aligned himself next to other great players (Wade, Bosh), by looking years ahead—when he was younger—making sure they would all free up from their contracts at the same time. In a matter of months great players caused upper level management to panic. Billionaires lost tons of money, GMs and coaches alike were fired, and the market changed forever. Players recognized their own self-worth. These players knew that their market moved based off the decisions they made, not the decisions of others around them. No matter how many rings he will attain, LeBron will be accredited to a movement.

In business, you need to become the best player, market your skills and initially sell them short-term to the highest bidder—or create your own_____. The short-term sell is significant. Often there will be all types of pressures to keep you in one realm. Find what you like, find what works for you, and pursue it. This is just an exaggerated example, but the point is to make work, work for you. If have been working in a field for an extended period of time and you feel as though you have outgrown your position, then it is time to take action. No one else will do it for you. If you are working for someone and they are getting your all, while shorting you financially and politically in the organization, then it is to their advantage to continue. It is nothing personal, usually, but it is good business. It is capitalism. What you must remember is that *the best of anything is prosperous.* The best custodian, construction worker, or factory worker are all prosperous. These three are considered blue collared jobs, but if a person is the best in any of those fields they can still be extremely prosperous. People want the best around them, and if you being around can benefit the organization pragmatically or superstitiously (even the morale or climate), then the organization will do whatever is necessary to keep you.

Many times other people or organizations know your own self-worth before you do. There are a few people, a small group, who want to help you grow and develop, but many are selfish and want you to themselves. At the end of the day, it *seems* to be good business to keep you. If you have ever had to move on from anything, and you received undeservingly negative feedback for leaving, then most likely that person or organization knew they were losing something good. If someone's reason for you staying in your same situation is because you cannot succeed on your own, then it is clear, they do not want to lose you. These people either cannot express that in an appropriate way or they do not fully understand your worth. Usually they know your worth because if they did not think you could survive on your own, then they would not want you on their team or want to have any type of association with you. Organizations do not want losers around and when they do not want you, they will get rid of you.

In relation to self-worth, most people are getting swindled. Companies play on people fears, and use [1]areas of opportunity to entice them into situations. Some organizations are no different than the shady looking character in a windowless van, politely offering free candy. Instead of just merely preying on your agnosticism, they go after what scares the hell out of you, your livelihood. Some fears many people have are not being able to retire at a reasonable age, a steady income, or [2]"job security." The essential fear, the "it" for companies, large and small alike, is your fear of taking risk. Companies know they have employees with families, personal needs, and so on. They know unless you find another job, which is incredibly tough

---

[1] Instead of calling it a weakness, the statement "areas of opportunity" is substituted. People must understand things are only a weakness if you accept it as that. Furthermore a weakness can be something you are not good at and may not necessarily need to be. It is being honest and realistic with yourself. If you want to improve in something you are not strong in it is considered an area of opportunity. Case in point, a professor might not be the best soccer player. Maybe after all the hours they spend studying and teaching they became a weak runner. So the professor could say they are weak at soccer. This has no effect on their craft. An area of opportunity would be something they need to improve on in their domain. Many students fail this said professor's course. As a SL the professor may look at himself and realize he has an area of opportunity. To better effectively communicate the lesson plan so more students can understand and progress. You are weak at things in which you have never had or don't have any business in. You just need improvement in things that directly impact you or your line of work. Later the guide will examine why the words you use in dialogue, such as this, are so significant.

[2] Job security in its own right is a thing of the past. America is a capitalistic society and with examples such as the Big Three, in automotives, "secure" corporations—companies, jobs, what have you—have already displayed their own interest and lack of fear of taking risks by outsourcing labor and straight forwardly laying off long-term employees some years, even months, before their "retirement package" kicks in. For them it saves money and it seems to be a good business move.

with the economic status of nations today, no matter how bad things are—you will not be going anywhere. Instead they unload more hours and more work on you, and you begin to stay busy. So busy that you do not have time to apply to other jobs, go to interviews, [3]socialize with people outside of work—who may have amazing career opportunities. Before you know it, you will find yourself on the "rat wheel." After enough time, you find yourself conforming. You give up because you feel emotionally beat, physically drained, and society trained. Trained to know what your supposed role is and the thought of leaving that place, no matter how bad it is, is a thought too heavy to bear. Realize this, *everything you want is on the other side of that fear*..everything.

The latter way you get cheated is by a common area of opportunity many people possess. It is a nasty habit all people have, to some degree, employed and unemployed alike. Complacency. In some aspect or another people become complacent in life. Whether through perceive happiness in your current situation or through the loss of willpower that comes after continuous setbacks and has finally caused you to give up or give in. A SL never becomes complacent. It is not the way; it is not what a SL does or is even capable of doing. If you give a SL $10 million, their next thought will sound something like this, "hmm if I can get 10, I definitely can get $20 million."

---

[3] Just the socializing aspect that jobs snatch away from you is profound. The saying, "it's not always what you know, but who you know," is true on a multitude of levels. It does not matter if you are a genius, if you don't know the right people to get your foot in the appropriate door, you will not flourish.

This is not to say don't appreciate life or enjoy happiness when it comes, it is just a subtle reminder to keep you successful.

When people become complacent they cannot become successful because success involves reaching your maximum potential and you are never done growing. Remember, the majority of this guide and set examples are tailored to those who do not want to run on the rat wheel. Those who would much rather work on their own schedule and do things their way. It is possible to ascend in a great organization and begin to do things your way (which is also the better and best way for the organizations success) or you can choose to branch out on your own. The important thing to take from this is literally, *you can do whatever you want.*

For example, let's say you are a small business banker for a prominent bank, making a base salary of $75,000 a year. You are showing outstanding potential and you know the ends and outs of what you are doing. However, your $75,000 is not even a fraction of the profits the bank is turning. You yourself have become accustomed to sealing million dollar deals and commission on these deals are around $2000—on the high end. While you are developing as a banker, you are not developing as a person and economically you are losing money. Instead of being happy with $75,000 (complacent), let's assess your self-worth. You are good at business, accounting, electronics—you learned to fix video games and computers from an old friend, you have a keen interest in basketball—you played through high school, then studied the game for fun as you aged, and through your banking experiences you have a network of friends and associates who are all business professionals. It turns out you are only using one of your many talents, the business accounting. The bank knows this and incorporates things into contracts such as making any external consulting gigs [4]illegal and making you sign non-disclosure agreements for the training you receive. American society teaches people to specialize. Becoming the best in one thing and working in that niche to get paid. However, this is a paradox to your uniqueness. You are good at many things, why not get paid using all of them. Instead of using 40plus hours a week on one or two skills for [5]another person, why not put that same amount of time into getting better at all your skills and making them work for you.

The bank itself does a variety of things, and has a variety of workers in different fields. The owner made a business, and makes money by having people do all the things they are good at. Personal banking, business banking, loans, you name it. Metaphorically you are maintaining another person's home. You are doing this for two reasons. The first being, you have not been exposed to the idea that you can make more money

---

[4] On a larger scale banks pay people to lobby in their interest for laws and create groups that offer licenses, and without the licenses giving financial advice is essentially illegal. They are paying for a competitive edge, just in case someone is bold enough to start their own small business.

[5] The point here is to make calculated moves so they are not considered risk. Work for others for a while, learn the business of things, continue to grow yourself, and start/continue to save your money. When the time is right, you give yourself the option to depart and strike out on your own. If you leave on a good note, go out and do well/learn more, you will always be welcomed back into a company, most likely with better pay and more autonomy. Look at some of Goldman Sachs top executives. Many have worked at different levels in the company, left and started their own businesses, or left and worked at other places (U.S. Treasury Dept.), and came back to higher bonuses, and autonomous positions.

doing things yourself, and the second is it is easier to maintain another home then build your own. In layman terms would you rather rent out a house for the rest of your life or have your own plow of land and your own house on top of it to reside in? A SL will quickly say the latter. Renting makes things easier. It is external. It is the quick fix, but it does not last. Sure when you rent you have a sense of wellbeing and support because if anything goes terribly wrong, you can get help. That is a great feeling. When you rent someone else meets all of your basic needs. What will happen if the landlord wakes up one day and want the place back, or even worse wants to sell it? There is nothing you can do, period. Sure there are contracts, but there are ways to get out of them. You don't have the knowledge, connections, or purse to challenge the landlord. Why you are just a renter. It is no different in business. If you rent long-term, you are putting your livelihood at a risk daily.

Take the tough route early, it will only make you stronger and later on you will appreciate everything you have worked for. In relation to business, work to increase your self-worth and get compensated for what your self is worth. After sitting down one day and writing all the knowledge, skills, and abilities, the banker possess, they will realize their self-worth is a lot more than what they are getting paid. Factoring in the going rates for things such as financial consultation (which they are qualified to do), electronic repairs—with the "ring of death" being popular with Xboxes, and youth basketball camps—the going rate on summer camps is absolutely ridiculous, it turns out people will pay good money to make sure their kids are safe and learning something, the banker realizes they are worth an easy $150,000 a year minimum. That is double the amount they are making working at a bank and tending to someone else's home. Using their business mind, the banker can turn these jobs into an actual business under one roof and most of their overhead will become tax-exempt. So not only is the banker pulling in tons of money, but they are also getting some of the money back from the government for starting a business. It is a win-win. The banker is providing quality services, doing all the things they love, and working on their own time. This is in part what makes a SL. Reaching your maximum potential.

A SL works at an accelerated pace. Your self-worth should be re-evaluated and updated every three months, four times a year. Record this information into your planner. When the time comes for you to ask for a raise, a contract, whatever the case may be you can present this information and have a valid argument.

> "You have greatness within you. You have gifts and talents you have been bestowed with and you must work consciously to make a determined deliberate effort to cultivate and bring them out."

Chapter 2

WHAT IS YOUR PURPOSE

If a person knows the true meaning of their existence on this earth they will never need to worry. When you know your purpose, you live every day, almost every minute toward completing that purpose. No matter what the rest of the world says or thinks, you know your actions are justified because it is an action supporting your purpose. It is human nature and it is the nature of a SL, the feeling of completion, the itch that needs to be scratched. People are passionate about needs, and this is what a purpose requires. Whether legitimate or not, a person's purpose satisfies their personal desires about why they wake up and try at this thing called life. Those without purpose cannot be a SL. It is impossible because they are not filling that requirement of passion. People without purpose have no direction and while often doing positive things, they are capricious. These people are not a good bet because in high stress situations they will quit. They will resort to doing what works best for them and if there was no purpose guiding them, then it is no reason for them to remain strained.

SLs care. They want something to be done right. SLs are willing to go the extra mile to make sure they understand what right is. If you were building a new home for you and your family, a home in a place you want to raise your children in, and have them do the same for their children and so forth, would you use cheap building materials? Would you not put the time and effort into researching the right company for the job, the right materials needed, the right neighborhood for the home, and so forth? This is something that matters to you; this is something that must be done right. This is the same feeling people have when their life's purpose is involved. Your purpose makes everything you do personal.

SL's often *think, reflect, plan, and act* upon their purpose. How often do you reflect? Not think. There is a distinct difference in the two. You think about what you want for lunch today. Thinking can be done while you are running errands around town. Reflection should occur when you are somewhere quiet and peaceful. Often times when you reflect, that bright light bulb above your head starts to illuminate. Hindsight is twenty-twenty for a reason. Hindsight occurs when you actually reflect on an event that has transpired. If you were to reflect before experiences, you can habitually have better outcomes. However reflection does require time and that is a luxury.

You cannot become the best you and reach your full potential if you do not know how to *reflect*. Reflecting upon yourself is often perplexing and difficult to do because people do not properly self-assess themselves. Think about the thing in your life that is most precious. Assuredly you spend time pondering about it. How to make it better or how to have more. This can be your relationships with family and friends, material things, or things of monetary value. The things you really care about in life and the things that take some work, also take thought. A couple of hours should be put aside at the beginning of every week to reflect. During this time, recognize accomplishments, time wasted, methods that work, and areas needed to improve on from the previous week. A thought is over in a moment's notice. One minute and thirty seconds. Reflection can last for days if not weeks.

Religious extremist may be the best group to observe when looking for an example of purpose. Extremist say their purpose is to spread _____'s word. Even though it is a tremendous purpose the statement is elementary, so you must explore why. This is reflecting. A SL would approach this purpose as such, "what makes me care who—if any—people worship?" "What am I getting out of spreading this message? Do I really believe I will get what I aim for? Is this purpose actually possible to complete and if not do I believe in it enough to die before its completion?" These are all the questions you should ask yourself when understanding what your purpose is in life. Next the SL will sit down and write an actual game plan to accomplish this purpose in the most [1]*3E* way. This game plan goes far beyond you as an individual. It puts a system in place, not a person. This way even in your absence, your purpose is still being fulfilled—if others feel it is valid. The final test of your purpose and your discipline of being a SL is how you act

---

[1] The three E (3E) approach compels you to question your course of action. Was this action *ethical, effective, and efficient?* Was the process morally right, was it completed, is there a better way of doing this? Take the 3E approach in every action you do in life. This *life compass* will become second nature to use as it guides you on the path to prosperity.

upon this purpose. Do you practice what you preach or are you fooling the person in the mirror?

"The idea. The idea is what separates SLs and the hoi polloi."

Chapter 3

PASSION AS PROPULSION

Your passion is that reservoir of untapped potential that usually only comes out in extreme circumstances. Find your purpose and you will find you are able to apply that passion to everything you do. Whether this is your children, your thirst for a better lifestyle or helping a community where you are from, formally identify your purpose and that passion will follow. A single mother of two, who decides to work a double shift every day, catching the bus from one job to another, is not propelled by the job or money it pays. She is propelled by the thought of providing for her family and making sure her children grow up with opportunities she may have not been afforded. She does not spend her hard earned cash on a new car, or a pair of shoes, she spends her money on her children. One child, in advanced placement classes for math, needs after school tutoring sessions and the other child needs cleats and camps for soccer. The situation is different for everyone, but you get the picture. She begins to invest in their future. The mother works hard every day because the passion she has to see her kids excel motivates her in a way money or status cannot begin to. Find your purpose and your passion will follow. You will find controlling that passion, that fire in your belly, in a professional manner will be harder than drawing upon it.

Shrewd businessmen, athletes, and warriors, if it is one thing they all have alike is the fact these people all recognize their passionate (assertive) side. All these people in their associated fields understand how effective their passionate methods are, but only the skilled can control it. For the warrior, the "whole man concept" is preached. The whole man concept lies in the ability to fight wars, speak at embassies in diplomatic fashions, then returning home to be a good parent and spouse. The athletes and business folks have a similar attitude. Punish any and all opposition or competition, display their professional side for the press and public, then put work to the side, go home, and perform their appropriate role in the family. These fields exemplify what a "on and off" switch is supposed to resemble. The "on and off" switch are common terms used to describe *attacking a situation*. When you turn the switch on, you are in that passionate mode accomplishing extraordinary things at an extraordinary pace. When you turn the switch off, you are calm.

The whole man concept means that any tactician, in their given field, must fully excel and master their work. If you are a SL, you are always a SL, in every part of your life. In all fields it is a matter of livelihood. If life at home or in the public distracts you from your work, and you cannot do your job, you are not worth anything in society, and you have no means to provide for yourself or others.

Just as a warrior will put their all into what they are doing because their life depends on it, you must put your all into your career because your livelihood does depend on it. Fighting the war is doing your job, passionately. Next is putting on your formal dress and integrating into society. Your business is just a part of you, not the whole you. There must also be room to go out into the public and become a SL in the community. Charities, volunteer work, or communicating your business to the public are all important things you must know how to do. Some media outlets are infamous for hassling those who do not want to talk. Those who either cannot or do not want to share any information about their business to the public. Be able to calmly communicate your thoughts about work or other aspects of life.

Finally it is going home and being a family figure. For all very talented and successful people this is the most difficult because reaching great levels at work consumes you. By the time you get home you are tired and it is hard to separate from your work. This is however an aspect of the whole man that cannot be skipped over. Live for and through your family. You must still go home and be the person your spouse married and the best parent possible to your children. Or for singles, still provide a shoulder for your friends to lean on and an opportunity for you yourself to unwind. At the end of the day this is why society keeps maturing and improving, for people.

To illustrate passionate work, look at how nasty political debates can become. Professional men and women resort to shouting, name-calling, blaming, and in some countries even fighting to get their point across. This is because all of these people are passionate—and because political discourse is important for growth. They believe in what they are fighting for and they have a purpose. When they discuss topics relative to their purpose sometimes their "opposition" can hit a nerve and cause someone to react in such a way they normally would not. Think about your physical state when you are mad. Maybe you get hot, shaky, you have tunnel vision and all you care about is what is in front of you at the time. You are no longer hungry, sleepy, or distracted. You feel invincible. Your eyes are on the target of your aggression. Now imagine that same focus in a professional state. When you are working with passion, this is what you can—will—bring to the table every day, all day. The whole man concept is about having that on and off switch and attacking your task. Passion is the energy associated with that switch.

"You gotta have reasons to get up when life knocks you down."

Chapter 4

WHAT IS YOUR MISSION STATEMENT

Your purpose is why you exist. Your mission statement is your constitution for life, and expression of your vision as well as values. Your purpose says where you walk to, while your mission statement states how you walk. Purpose is all mental and your mission statement is something concrete. There is no right or wrong mission statement and it is possible for your mission statement to change over time as you develop as a person. The important thing is that you have one. Look at any fortune 500 company or successful business. The company and their leaders all have some sort of mission statement. Whether it is short, long, or "cliché," they all have one. This is because these things work, they are proven to work. Write a statement about your mission. Relate your mission statement to your purpose, they should align and run parallel for the most part.

Your personal mission statement will force you to be accountable to the one SL that should have one of the highest standards—yourself. Your purpose should be written in a personal manner, but a mission statement should be written with a relationship to those who follow you (a SL does have followers). It should exemplify the purpose, guide decision making, and spell out its overall goal, while providing a sense of direction for you as a SL and the organizations for which you represent. These organizations are often family, friends, and co-workers. The mission statement should provide the framework for which the organizations strategies are formulated. If honesty is a part of your mission statement, and a situation occurred where lying may bring a more suitable outcome than the truth, your decision should still be one of integrity. The mission statement is for long-term success, not for wins in every isolated incident. Your mission statement looks at life as a marathon, not a sprint, and if you want to finish the race in the place you have set as a goal, you should formulize your strategy in a mission statement and follow it.

YouTube's mission statement is to provide fast and easy video access and the ability to share videos frequently. Short and direct. By the mission statement described, leaders in the YouTube organization most likely promote decisions that will enhance the speed of video access and video sharing. How about a more complex mission statement? "The Ritz-Carlton hotel is a place where the genuine care and comfort of our guest is the highest mission. We pledge to provide the finest personal service and facilities for our guest who will always enjoy a warm, relaxed, yet refined ambiance. The Ritz-Carlton experience enlivens the senses, instills well-being, and fulfills even the unexpressed wishes and needs of our guests." This is the mission statement of the Ritz-Carlton hotel. Here the mission statement is longer than the previous and it hits on a plethora of values the Ritz-Carlton has. The general population may not know the people of this company personally, but through their mission statement people can form assumptions.

In summary, the first sentence ensures everything the hotel does, all the changes it will make in the future are for the care and comfort of the guest. They want people to know the Ritz-Carlton is honestly concerned with the treatment of their guest while staying at their hotels. The second sentence gets even more personal with guests. Not only is the Ritz-Carlton going to ensure you are treated properly, but they will be attentive to every guest's each individual need—"finest personal service." Last, the Ritz-Carlton has also made it their mission to guarantee an experience and anticipate and fulfill everything a guest might need or want. This hotel has made it its mission to ensure their guest are each personally cared for above and beyond ways they expect and leaving with the hotel's image imprinted into their mind as an experience. Events are supposed to be experiences. Theme parks, museums, sporting events, are all things you can go do and remember the experience for the rest of your life. Hotels traditionally are a place you stay maybe on the way to one of those events, but the Ritz-Carlton places their hotels in the same category by telling their guest, the Ritz-Carlton will be an experience. Think about how that makes you feel as a consumer. To know someone has a mission to put that much time and effort into you. It is no wonder why the Ritz-Carlton is such a popular and well sought after hotel for overnight stay and if that is not enough they have unintentionally coined a popular word for opulence in today's culture "ritzy." They *don't take short cuts and they do things the right way.*

The lengths of mission statements do not matter. It can be direct and to the point or it can be pages long ensuring it hits on every point and value the person or organization has. Many mission statements in companies are found on a placard somewhere in a common space where everyone can see it daily. While you might not want your mission statement to be that public, it should be somewhere where you can repeatedly refer to it. Keep it on the first page of your planner, on your fridge, the bathroom mirror, or all three. Just have it placed somewhere you can consistently see it. Know your mission statement by heart, so if you were asked it (or a variation of it) you can immediately and effectively communicate what you represent. Remember, you want things to be second nature and the only way for this to occur is to *get accustomed to seeing it, saying it, and doing it*. A liar lies because they are used to lying. It is embodied in them. It gets to a point where they can't help but to lie whether it brings them good fortune or not. Get personal with your mission statement and get used to living your life off the words written and before you know it, it will become second nature.

"Never compromise your ultimate ambition, no matter how distant the vision may be."

Chapter 5

WHAT IS PROSPERITY

People in some places count the years they live as prosperous, other places count cows, the amount of children you have, or the amount of money you have attained.

Sometimes people are so blinded by becoming monetarily rich; they don't realize how much they have to give up getting there. There are very few millionaires who did not put in the time to match the dollar. Usually it is time loss spending with family and loved ones—which can be critical on relationships, tremendous amounts of stress on your body and mind, or life/death risk taking activities.

To further explore the concept of success, one must clearly define the meaning of money. The meaning of money is not anything anyone should let be dictated to them. While money is significant, the weight placed on it should not be the same as your purpose. We cannot live without eating, but we don't live to eat. [1]Always remember what money is in the literal sense. It is paper, and it is worthless. Money is merely a note saying you possess something valuable, but for whatever reason you cannot carry it around. It is the same as a debit card. A debit card is a piece of plastic, but because you have more money than you can carry, for safety reasons or because reasons of wealth, you present a plastic card in exchange. If an apocalyptic war were to occur and the world was left in shambles, the man with the healthy cow would be more valuable than any dollar. The ideal of money exist because as a society we believe in the weights that have been placed on it. You must define what the dollar is worth to you. Determine the value of money by adding how much it will take to accomplish your purpose, as well as take care of the needs and wants of you and your family. Set a realistic number for yourself and thoroughly seek out why this number is what it is.

When famous comedian Dave Chappelle, turned down a 50plus million dollar deal to continue to do his show on Comedy Central, people thought Dave went crazy. Speculations occurred in which some said Dave was smoking crack, or that he was in a mental institution, and so on. In reality none were true. The famous comedian went away to Africa to just be himself. When Dave returned to America and gave his reasoning on various talk shows, some people were still blinded

---

[1] Looking at something in a different light such as this is merely to train a brain to do it on a regular basis on its own. Having your own devil's advocate will help in life by being able to see every aspect from every angle and making an educated decision without the formal training. This is one of the many invaluable qualities of a SL.

by the money and not his purpose as a man. Dave explained he enjoyed making people laugh. Yes he, like others, need to get paid for his services to live, but if the money intervened with his purpose it was not worth it. On a televised interview, Inside the Actors Studio, Dave told the audience when he graduated high school he had a talk with his father about being a comedian/actor. Dave's father told him that everyone might not make it in the comedic/acting world. Dave told his father it depends on what making it is. His father responded by asking Dave what was "making it" to him. Dave said to his father that if he could make more than a teacher's salary—with his father being a teacher—doing comedy, then he would have made it. Dave's father told him to name his price in the beginning, and if it ever got more expensive than the price he named then to get out of there (there being the business), "thus Africa." Dave stated after two successful seasons of the highly rated and record breaking "Chappelle's show" of doing it his way, the third season in which he was offered the $50 million, Dave was asked to do his comedy different. The producers wanted Dave to do comedy sketches and say "comedic" things that he did not agree with. In addition, Dave stated that he is a "people person" and after it became public about the kind of money he stood to make on the third season, people started to look at him different and treat him different. In one instance he jokingly said the way two cartoon characters sit around and one starts to get hungry, then looks at the other and imagines them as a chicken, is the same way people were starting to look at him. Instead of taking the money, selling his soul, and not living for his purpose, Dave decided to get away from it all and go to Africa, where the people saw him as just another ordinary guy, not some sort of famous star.

What is your purpose? How can you turn that purpose into a business or find an existing business to work for to integrate living your life the way you want and make a decent living to support yourself or your family? Think about how many kids you want one day, where you would want to live, what you would want to drive, and so on. What is the number that will make you happy? Sure if a time came when you could exceed that number and still have purpose in life and in your work then by all means continue. However, if you find yourself one day miserable at work, especially after you have met and exceeded your planned number, then it may be time to find something else to do. Don't go out and quit your day job, or make a significant decision without any alternatives—paying dues is a part of life's journey, but remember everyone will only get one life, do not waste it being miserable every day.

Becoming Prosperous

1. **Decide to be Prosperous.**
   - Look at how much you are worth quarterly.
2. **Get Rid of Fast Food Mentality.**
   - Organizations want SLs and you should and will be rewarded accordingly for everything you do. There is a reason why people make mansions and buy islands. There is a reason why people have what seems to be an excessive

amount of money, because there is an excessive amount of money out there and it is not going away.

3. **Treat it Like a Duty.**

- Prosperous people are motivated not just by money, but by a need for the marketplace to validate their contributions. SLs don't lower their targets when things get tough. Rather, they raise expectations for themselves because they see the difference they can make with their families, organization and community.

4. **Surround Yourself with Like Minded People.**

- It is difficult to stay motivated and learn new things when you do not surround yourself with people who are attempting to do the same. You need to know what people are doing to create prosperity and follow their example: What do they read? What drives them? How do they stay motivated and excited?

5. **Work Like Your Life Depends on It.**

- SLs are consumed by their hunt for success and work to the point they feel they are winning and not just working.

6. **Shift Focus from Spending to Investing.**

- The wealthy don't spend money; they invest.

7. **Create Multiple Flows of Income.**

- Prosperous people never depend on one flow of income, but instead create a number of revenue streams. Unlock your inner hustle. Hustling is one of those sleek urban words you may only expect to hear from some rapper or trendy youth in the inner city. However hustle holds volume. Hustling is simply diversifying your portfolio in real time. The same way you can have stocks in different companies, bonds, mutual funds, retirement portfolios, etc. is the same way the hustle works. Different ways of creating income for yourself simultaneously. Implementing all that you are good at into businesses. The Chase bank employee in Ch. 1 becomes a hustler if they strike out on their own. Fixing games, financial advising, and summer camps. All those are forms of a hustle. It is okay to hustle, unlock it and embrace it. What corporation or business do you know that only does one thing? There are not many one trick pony's for a reason. So if fortune 500 companies diversify what services they are capable of providing, why would you not follow suit? The "hustle and bustle" of the city is a common phrase that has a profound meaning. In metropolitan cities something is always going on, someone is always working. The coming and going, nonstop buzzing around is for a reason, people are hustling. What are your hustles?

"You must learn new ways to think."

Chapter 6

FAILURE IS JUST A PRICE TO PAY TO ACHIEVE SUCCESS

Failure as a Process

Always remember failure is purely subjective. It is based off of your expectations. In addition, like success, failure is a process. You can't become successful overnight, nor can you fail overnight. When BP was attributed for the notorious Deepwater Horizon/Gulf oil spill, in 2010, fingers were pointed in every direction. While the oil spill certainly was the failure, all the top executives, researchers, and government officials knew that that wasn't the actual problem. The problem was *how* did this happen. Failures are the effect, problems are the cause. BP blamed the accident on a variety of serious problems that caused the spill. Some problems included: mechanical failures (many machines were not being maintained properly), human error/judgments, engineering design, operational implementation, and team interfaces. The oil spill didn't just suddenly happen, there is documented evidence a process happened first. After the crisis, an abundance of literature was written on oil spills. Some of which included: how to prevent oil spills, how to clean up oil spills, emergency plans, crisis communication, etc. The company and the world became better post spill because people learned lessons from their mistakes. From problems, the consequence is either success or failure. Failure is the accumulation of events and decision making that led to an unfavorable outcome. Set your own goals and expectations so you can decide what is failing or not. Go over these in the workplace with peers, subordinates, and superiors so everyone has a clear understanding of expectations.

Failure for Personal Growth

You will fail. As soon as you understand this, succeeding will become that much easier. Failure is a rite of passage for a SL. It is something that brings them all together. Striving to reach your maximum potential of any craft in life, will inevitably lead to failures of some sort. No one is perfect. On the path to success, failure will simply expose to you what processes work and which one's do not. Make failure your ally. It is worth just as much to know when you will fail as it is to succeed. The more you fail early on, the less likely it is to happen later on in life. Your cognitive memory allows you to learn from your mistakes and to recognize potential new ones from previous experiences.

Failure allows you to see what doesn't work. Leadership positions usually take a while to get, but they are easy to lose. When you are in charge of people and organizations, their threshold for mistakes is low. People expect their leaders to have already had the training and experience to lead everyone else. This is where knowing ineffective processes are important. Over the years and after many tried and tested methods you should be able to better shape your decision making process, already having an abundance of information stored from previous encounters.

For example, a grease fire starts in a culinary student's kitchen and they try to put it out with water, the flames ignite more. Their professor calmly grabs a few items, walks over and puts it out. From that experience the student learns to smother the flames with baking soda and to put a metal lid on top of the fire. If you are in the business of cooking, fires will occasionally occur. Since this person failed early on in life and learned a valuable lesson they are more likely to succeed when it occurs again. Embrace failures.

Regardless how trivial, a SL can give a person many examples of failure, but look at what separates them from the mediocre individual. At the end of a failure story a SL will give you the lesson or perhaps the motivation that was gathered from it. Despite how critical or petty, there are lessons to be learned. For example, you let someone borrow twenty dollars and they intentionally never return it. Many people may look at this and say it's just twenty bucks it is not a big deal and in the big scheme of life it isn't. Now scratch the surface. You failed to recognize this person's low level of integrity and it caused you to make a bad decision. This doesn't mean not to trust anyone, but it does say this same individual is untrustworthy. A SL takes a life lesson, some people don't keep their word and if a person is capable of doing it for *something trivial then they are definitely capable of doing it at a larger scale*. In essence the

31

message is this, whatever you deem a mistake or consider a failure in life (not just in the workplace) learn something from it and become a better you. You never know when a similar situation with more severe consequences may occur.

Six random ideas that will help you fail better, more often and with an inevitably positive upside:

1. Whenever possible, take on specific projects.
2. Make detailed promises about what success looks like and when it will occur.
3. Engage others in your projects. If you fail, they should be involved and know that they will fail with you.
4. Be really clear about what the true risks are. Ignore the vivid, unlikely and ultimately non-fatal risks that take so much of your focus away.
5. Concentrate your energy and will on the elements of the project you have influence on, ignore external events you can't avoid or change.
6. When you fail (and you will) be clear about it, call it by name and outline specifically what you learned so you won't make the same mistake twice. People who blame others for failure will never be good at failing, because they've never done it.

"The fellow who never makes mistakes takes his orders from one who does." -Herbert V. Brocknow-

Chapter 7

THE PATH TO SUCCESS

The hardest thing for SLs to understand is why everyone else wouldn't want the same kind of life. A chance to be autonomous, respected, and make a decent living—at the same time doing something you love. Imagine your dream vacation. For some it's the Caribbean. Nice warm beaches, clear waters, exceptional dining, friendly people, etc., it's a remarkable trip many would want. You decide you want to take this trip with a group of your friends. Months in advance you lay out the cost and travel arrangements. However a week or so before your supposed departure many of your friends bail out. Some don't have the money to fully pay for the trip, some did not think you were serious about taking such a big trip, others feel it is too much work involved in getting there and back and would rather stay somewhere local, the reasons vary. Everyone wants a vacation, but everyone does not take the necessary steps to have one.

The same thing happens in business and on the path to prosperity. Many people have the million dollar thoughts with a minimum wage attitude. While becoming successful and prosperous is not impossible, it does take some hard work. SLs understand what it takes to reach the top and with a common complaint of people today being their career status, one would think they invest the time to progress themselves. As you climb the ladder in life you may want your friends, family, and close associates to join you. You may say to those close to you, that the current week is one for work not partying. Or perhaps you are saving your money for a bigger venture down the line. While this sounds good to you professionally, everyone might not be on the same page. While those close to you may or may not accept and respect your decisions with your goals, majority of them definitely will not follow suit. People traditionally do what they want. So instead of having everyone you grew up with surround you professionally, you end up with newfound friends and yourself. Usually yourself at the beginning of your career. The next book will mold you to be ready to take on the toughest challenges, many of which involve you.

Many times, most people have two separate sets of friends. Those who have worked full-time in very professional environments have already realized this. One set of friends are your personal ones. These are the people you grew up with, family members, and the people you really are yourself with. You can use your traditional dialect, accent, and wear whatever you want around them because they know you for you. The problem with these people in business however is the conflict of interest. If you decide to work with them, they may not always respect your knowledge in business areas because of your behavior on a personal level. In essence they cannot let go of who you used to be, or they cannot separate the professional business and personal side of your life. To them you are still "little Johnny" or whatever other moniker you were ascribed growing up. This is an issue when "little Johnny" is now Jonathan what-have-you, in charge of some corporate business, where your stock is plummeting and you are fighting a public relations battle to restore confidence in the organization. However your friend or family member may not fully see you in the serious position you are in and continues to publically joke around with you. What you two might feel is harmless and business as usual, is perceived to investors as a sign of immaturity and a red flag on leadership (regardless of age and experience). These same friends may also not have the drive, discipline, or competence you do to reach their full potential. Here you are left with the choice of putting your purpose to the side to fulfill someone else's (which if their purpose is legitimate enough, there is nothing wrong with doing this), or continuing along your path and fully knowing these friends are great to have around in your free time, but not in the workplace. Support your friend(s) business transition or remove them from your life. Transition them by training and bringing them up to speed professionally, or get rid of them.

The second set of friends you will have are your business associates. You may not meet these people until your late 20s, 30s, 40s, and so on. However, to ensure expedient successful business transactions and keep levels of trust high in organizations, you must also be able to have friendly, honest, and deep discussions with these people. After a while you develop relationships with anyone in close proximity for extended periods of time. SLs keep all relationships either on a close intimate level or professional, but better results are achieved when they are intimate so aim high. [1]These friends will be the people that introduce you to different things in life, become great references for careers, and great team members because they are just as competitive and hopefully as ethical as you are. In the workplace they can be trusted, thus making them trustworthy even in a personal sense. Both sets of friends will have similar characteristics. Many times in tight knitted communities these two even overlap, which is fine as long as everyone knows to play their roles accordingly at the appropriate time. The transitions between both groups of friends happen as you grow and strive to reach your maximum potential in life.

The path to prosperity. While it is a straight path, it is often cold, lonely, and hard to climb. Many will not want to do it, regardless of the reward. This can be due to their lack of internal competencies (no discipline or drive) or external factors which have prevented them (children, life purpose shifting, ailing

---

[1] Business associates come from all walks of life. Their different upbringings and cultures will allow you to experience new things in life that may not have been feasible dealing with people you have known. This is often very helpful later in your career when you continue to work with new people, and being knowledgeable in different areas of life perceives you as all the more competent. For example, decide to spend some holidays with a coworker or classmate instead of your own immediate circle. These people might be from another country, state, or just live life different in a cultural sense. Spend some time away from work or class with these people and learn something new. Later on in life if you do business with someone from that walk of life, who on first impression definitely do not expect you to have any knowledge on their culture and you share an anecdote or fun fact about it, watch how receptive they become. People love to talk about their own experiences and things they enjoy and if you can relate, the human element cannot be ignored. Sometimes this may be the difference between a job, promotion, and an opening in an organization where everyone insisted there was not any more room for new prospects.

family members). *You will not be able to force anyone along the path*; it is hard enough to do it on your own. Do not let this deter you. You must be ready and willing to make loneliness your best friend. The early mornings and late nights dedicated to your work is for you to become one step closer to attaining your purpose. Reach your full potential because if what you're doing now is good—you can become great, if you are great and you wish for more you can become a legend, a template example after you seemingly reach your full potential.

> "Greatness, everything before you is obsolete, and
> everything after has your mark."

BOOK II

LEADERSHIP

The pressure is on, the past does not matter at this point and it seems the decisions made now will influence all aspects of life after. In these situations, businesses, teams, organizations, etc. all ask the same question; who can we call on to get the job done? Critical times and moments reveal a lot about an organization. It is in these moments where new SLs are found, and the established ones continue to display and increase their extreme value. This is the time where the "overpaid" and "underworked" CEO must take the reins of a company, fix the problem and continue to lead the business into prosperity. Or when the star quarterback gets injured in the big game and his replacement comes in and excels. Whatever the case may be, the leader must rally everyone up and bring back *results not excuses*. Book II explores the mind-frame of a leader and how they impact those around them.

Leadership, in the rawest form, is determining what needs to be done in a situation and getting people to do it.

Chapter 8

WHO ARE YOU

When you begin to think for yourself and make decisions for yourself, ambiguity begins. Many people cannot admit they don't exercise this responsibility. Often times the media, agenda setters, work organizations, or community leaders influence your thoughts and steers your decision making without you even knowing it. Habitually, people blissfully give up their freedom and their earning potential in exchange for having someone else take responsibility for telling them what to do next! How much are you giving up?

The Paradox of Choice: Why More is Less, is a book from 2004 by Barry Schwartz, and it spells out this very notion. Psychologists, Mark Lepper and Sheena Iyengar, ran a very memorable social experiment. They set up—in a gourmet food store—a display featuring a line of exotic, high-quality jams, customers who came by could taste samples, and they were given a coupon for a dollar off if they bought a jar. In one condition of the study, 6 varieties of the jam were available for tasting. In another, 24 varieties were available. In either case, the entire set of 24 varieties was available for purchase. The large array of jams attracted more people to the table than the small array, though in both cases people tasted about the same number of jams on average. When it came to buying, however, a huge difference became evident. Thirty percent of the people exposed to the small array of jams actually bought a jar; only three percent of those exposed to the large array of jams did so.

Analysis paralysis is what frequently occurs when people are presented with so many options they are unable to make a choice, fearing they will make the wrong one. According to analysis paralysis, the brain (already over-worked and exhausted) cannot cope with too many choices. Being presented with too many options supposedly stresses the brain. It gives it too many things to compare and contrast, while not enough time to do the research.

This ambiguity occurs because people are not used to making decisions for themselves. You make the decision based off the options you are given, rarely questioning if more options are available. What is interesting about the jam study is that more people were attracted to the table with more jams. That alone confirms people inherently want choices and want the freedom to choose. However, once it is time to make that choice you panic. You start to over think things and remember what the outside world has told you what is suitable, not what you see things as right. When you are a SL there will be a ton of situations that become breeding grounds for ambivalence. As a result of *knowing who you are and what you aim to be* you will eliminate these vague times and go with the 3E approach. Trust in your decision-making and take actions flawlessly. Prize your independence and be who you tell yourself you will be.

Your identity must lie in who you are, not what you do. While what you do certainly intertwines into your thought pattern, never let it make you who you are. Frequently people in their given profession falter when their career is over, especially when that said career does not end on their terms. From the business men who commit suicide after a financial meltdown, to soldiers who return to their home country and cannot assimilate back into the normal population, or even the athlete who cannot let go of the glory they had during their playing days. The thing all these people have in common is that their identity rested in their title. You know people like this, everyone does. Many people have either seen or worked for that late night supervisor who is hell-bent on power or control and wants all of their employees to know who is boss. This type of person is not comfortable in their own skin. If the only reason you can garner respect is because of the position you are in or the title you hold, then there is a clear problem.

As a SL your value lies in who you are, what you can do, and more importantly what you have the potential to do. Know your identity, tell your story, and that will be enough to distinguish yourself from others. If it is genuine, people will love it. Title's will always come and go and to combat the sensation to attach yourself to one, just develop who you are. A title should be the icing on the cake, not the cake itself. Always remember everyone follows different leaders for different reasons. The identity, the story is what separates SLs and thus their following. In Christian churches majority of the preachers use the same bible, quote the same examples, and for the most part interpret the bible the same way. If this is the case then why are there so many preachers? This is because people are attracted to them for different reasons. A personal connection perhaps, or the way they look, possibly even the way the preacher speaks. Attracting different followers lies in the identity more than the title. Begin to look at yourself as the business and build your brand. Know who you are.

Take some time, reflect, and then answer these questions below to begin to form your identity.

What are you trying to achieve?

What are you willing to sacrifice?

What makes you happy, what doesn't?

What is your purpose?

What gets in the way?

What's important to you?

What isn't?

What are your pros and cons?

What are your copouts and what level of control do you have? (Read on)

"Knowing others is intelligence; knowing yourself is true wisdom. Mastering others is strength, mastering yourself is true power." -Lao-Tzu-

Chapter 9

EXCUSES, COP-OUTS, AND A WAKEUP CALL

People prematurely think they are living their life right. You think everything that happens to you is because of your bad luck and you are the only person in the world with problems. Your views, thoughts, and values are pessimistic. Not only do you not want to succeed, it aggravates and agitates you tremendously to see others do well or try to make something of themselves. Instead of giving them praise you look for justifications as to why someone is in the position they are in and why they will not stay there long, hopefully. It is the same sentiment that can be seen from the masses toward athletes, musicians, corporate executives, and entertainers. The amount of time, energy, and thought put into someone the masses have never met, will never meet, and never crosses the mind of the contradictory individual, is ridiculous. Do not turn into this being, ever. Everyone has had flashes where they have begun to say something negative or hateful for no apparent reason. When this happens, catch yourself, laugh at the mistake, explore the real issue, and then appropriately communicate your point of view. More times than not, the individual you do not actually know, has no direct impact on your life or the issue at hand. You yourself however can impact you and the world around you.

No one cares why you are late, why the job didn't get done, or why you are not focused, etc. Even those who listen don't care. People listen because they are too polite to walk off or cut you short. In the best-case scenario people may momentarily care, but in the fast pace world of today people don't have time to concern themselves with your issues. Everyone has enough stuff they have to keep up with in their own home and family, in their private personal life, and their particular community. Even those close to you who do take an interest in your situation, will stop worrying after they see you give up on yourself. No one wants to hold your hand through everything and as a SL you should not want that treatment. You should despise it. If issues keep surfacing around you it is for two reasons only. One, everyone knows you are the go to person to fix things, or two, you are the issue. For the sake of your livelihood don't be or become the latter.

Muammar Gaddafi, deceased prime minister/president of Libya, ruled for forty years. It does not matter how he ruled, his methods are not under scrutiny here. Take out all the intangibles and look at the raw data. One man, millions of people, forty years, an empire. If one man, can rule millions, for forty years, then there is no reason why you cannot lead the life you want, and become a master over yourself. There is no excuse: not to have the career you want, not to flourish with a team of individuals, not to become the SL of your relatively small realm compared to one of Gaddafi's. *Take control of your life* and go where you want with it.

> "When you are just complaining, then things
> aren't that bad yet."

Chapter 10

RELIEF OF LEADERS

The amount of military commanding officers that are relieved of duty each year because of their decision making is absurd. Not just their decisions regarding military matters, but more get relieved because of their decisions they made as an officer. "Failure unbecoming of an officer" is the official title for this leper that gets placed on these commanding officers. These people who are put in very high positions of trust abuse it all types of ways; from adultery, lying, sleeping with subordinates, discrimination, abuse of power, abuse of authority in the community or at work, and questionable integrity to name a few. Their lives are more scandalous than any television show or movie. This isn't just for military officers either. This behavior can be observed in politicians and "leaders" worldwide. Beloved coach [1]Joe Paterno was a modern man who had a statue built for him. Paterno's legendary 40plus year career became a staple in college society, not just for the football wins, but for what he believed in as a person. His symbol was tarnished and erased in one swoop by something he

---

[1] American college football coach who was the head coach of the Penn State Nittany Lions from 1966 to 2011.

did not even physically do, but for his lack of judgment as a leader. SLs are responsible for holding everyone under them accountable.

Are you in control of your plan and people? If not you have a dilemma. Companies today are firing employees, spokesmen, and ambassadors alike on the spot after they slip. Especially if that slip is public. Companies would rather pay out the rest of someone's contract and give them an early exit, than be associated with some sort of foul comment or offensive belief and behavior. Comedian and once Aflac duck's voiceover Gilbert Gottfried was fired immediately after he made insensitive remarks on [2]twitter about Japan's tsunami. With the new age of social media and the speed in which information can travel globally, Gottfried just joined a now already lengthy list of those who are dismissed from an organization because of their decision making.

---

[2] Recently many famous athletes, musicians, and actors have opened twitter accounts. Twitter is a medium to communicate and express what a person is doing during their day and how they are feeling. Each twitter account is allowed followers—users that can see what is written on another person's wall. It is a pretty addicting service. The issue however is that when stressful situations occur in people lives they take to their twitter account. They spew out everything they are feeling, good or bad, and it is uncensored. For the average user with a few hundred followers, this is not really a big deal; in fact it's an interactive journal or autobiography of sorts. It is actually a great way to get something off your chest in a controlled nonviolent environment. Businesses even take to their twitter accounts to express their politically correct stance to public issues. However, for the "famous" user (the musicians, athletes, actors, etc.) their openness is usually seen as unwanted rants, especially for the organization they work for or represent. Through twitter postings, news stories have erupted of these rants causing those with fame or those with thousands of followers, to lose not only endorsement deals, but their job as well. Afterwards these same people become the black sheep of their community.

People are not, will not let things slide. The amount of respect, power, and money that goes to the top tier people, leave everyone else only wanting one thing in return, results. They want a SL. Top tier success and leadership in your craft and as a human being. Nothing else is tolerated. Coaches, athletes, military leaders, politicians, businessmen, entertainers, no one is exempt and everyone, one day, is held accountable. Those foundations are laid because that is what will continue to make organizations and countries excel, and become everlasting—to cut out any cancer on an individual level or structural.

In your position you must make the tough decisions. It does no good to supplement someone because their eventual downfall, when that time bomb goes off, may take others—if not the whole organization with them. If you cannot convert someone to the discipline of a SL, treat them as a contagious sickness and stay away.

"Every action should be met with an action not a reaction, your response to circumstances are more important than the circumstance itself."

Chapter 11

WHY YOU SHOULD CHANGE

Whether you believe leaders are born or developed, one thing is certain, leadership is a craft. Like any craft it takes a certain amount of time studying, practicing, and testing to have some level of expertise or become a master. Some aspects of a leader may be present since birth, that doesn't mean you are ready to run a fortune 500 company though. Just because you are born with something, does not mean you will die with it, growth in everything is a continuous process. Some people are born with a silver spoon in their mouth and die poor. Others are the epitome of fit in their teenage and early adult years, and then become unhealthy adults. Or possibly the most common, the Young Turk, a belly full of fire, with changing the world on their radar, becomes the bitter and pessimistic middle aged adult.

The concept of change is constant throughout the guide. The thought of new paradigms you must acquire, "owning" a home instead of "renting," "rewiring your mental state," and so on. The bottom line is that you must understand you are an unfinished product. It is up to you to determine if you want to be an unfinished product with a 50,000 dollar value, or a million. If you have made it this far then it is apparent you are ready to alter your paradigms, your mindset, and grow. Changing involves putting aside your personal biases, researching the right way, and adapting to the methods involved.

It is very important to understand and have an appreciation for the FACT, that your mind, like your body is a tool. Athletes and soldiers take this appreciation to an extreme, but it can be seen in any ordinary job as well. To highlight how athletes and soldiers appreciate their body as a tool, observe how they carefully prepare and treat their body. These people constantly work out like their life depends on it—because it some circumstances it does, they stretch, spend the money on massages, eat healthy (in most cases), make a conscious effort to know what their body intakes before big events, and so on. In some instances, of fitness enthusiasts, they will not even entertain the idea they are eating for pleasure. They don't enjoy a meal, these people call it feeding. Simply feeding the machine, and in these cases the food does not need to be mouthwatering, juicy, or delicious. All the plate needs to have is the right mix of healthy fruits, vegetables, starches, carbs, etc. to help the body intake the highest level of fuel needed to excel. Majority of people don't realize their body is a tool, even less their mind, and in order to get work done that tool must be ready to operate at all times. If you have to get up and go to work every day your body is a tool being used as one of the most important weapons in your arsenal. It does you no good to be sick, sleepy, or lame. Look at how much importance a surgeon places on their hands. Surgeons know their hands are the things that brings them their livelihood, so they do everything to protect them. Simultaneously the "knife" the surgeon uses to operate with must also be sharp to be effective. Looking at your mind as a tool, appreciate the fact it must also be sharpened. You will not be effective and you will not prosper in today's world without a sharp refined mind.

Predominantly: athletes are not more valuable than the general manager, the construction worker is not as esteemed as the foreman, and the soldier does not have more command than the general; no matter how elite any of the foremost are considered. On average, the body will wear down before the mind and it is limited in how advanced it can become. Those who use their body primarily to make money and have no plans on one day converting that source of income to their mind, survive on a limited clock. Those who don't continue to refine their mind are also on a limited clock. [1]The thinker is much more valuable than the doer, primarily because it takes a shorter amount of time to train people to do things. Think of it this way, animals have been trained to do, replicate, repeat, human actions or follow and obey commands. People have been able to train animals on a wide spectrum. Dogs for example can be taught a variety of domestic commands, combative commands, or trained to sniff out drug paraphernalia and explosives. These are examples of the doer. No matter how "rich" someone seems, if they are using their body, there is usually someone, somewhere, at the organization in a better position. Possibilities for the mind are endless. Rational thought processes and creativity—just to name a couple—take more time to teach and

---

[1] Not to say the thinker has never been the doer—everyone has a start somewhere, but how many "wealthy" people do you see using their body to make money?

develop. In other words it takes longer for someone to comprehend why things are done, then to show them how things are done, which is why individuals in those positions who know "the why" are rewarded justly.

Using your mind will get you wealthy. Rich only provides for a while, while wealth last through generations. SLs are wealthy. Not always monetarily, it can be a wealth of experience or a wealth of knowledge, but they are wealthy. Mind over matter.

Every day people who are considered "experienced" are getting fired for the young college grad, who can be trained in the same thing quicker, already comes with new knowledge, and the ambition to help the company and themselves grow. A lot of people don't agree with this, especially older, but right now is the time to come to realization of your mistake. A company sees a twenty-year person who has worked hard as a good worker. This person did their job, well. They also see that in twenty years this person did not help the company GROW! In no way did they help expand their reach. This does not have to be economically (even though that is probably the most sought after). Expansion could be in the community, new technologies to speed up the way they do things, new ideas to change culture and climate for the better. [2]Anything to help develop and grow the company. All things that make you use your mind, not necessarily your body. Even to show signs that you have been attempting to grow yourself. The more you do this, the better

---

[2] If you help with the expansion of a company, more than likely you will be kept around because now you are assisting in writing the book on how things will be done in this new area of operation.

chance of you helping yourself open up new positions that were not previously available and putting yourself in a position where you are needed. After twenty years of working, you might think you have or had a career, but really it has just been a job. No matter how much you made, make, or your position, if you are being oust, it may have just been a job.

The single most powerful investment in life is investment in you. You will not always be allowed to rely on your past experiences, money, rank, or [3]who you know. You have to ensure you have yourself in check before you lead others. This can be subordinates or peers at work, or your own family and friends. Not only would you not follow someone who didn't know where they were going, but you cannot be comfortable leading people in an unfamiliar area. Become a better you. Be proactive in life and get things done.

"People who know how will always have a job, people who know why will always be the boss."

---

[3] When people are consistently "name dropping" it is a red flag. If a person is the best at what they are doing, they don't need to use other people names to validate themselves.

Chapter 12

HOW YOU SHOULD CHANGE

There are three simple things you must do to embrace change and evolve:

1. Know you need to. You must know how to be upfront and honest with yourself, and if that doesn't work listen to someone who can be upfront to you about your flaws. It is said the first step to any recovery is denial. No one wants to believe they need to get better or try different approaches at things. That is your ego and sense of pride talking to you.

2. Have a desire. Even if you know what you can work on to become a better person, a stronger SL, it doesn't matter if you don't actually want too. How many people still smoke to this day fully aware of the detrimental effects it has on their health? A box of cigarettes even states it contributes to cancer and death, but people still smoke packs a day. In the end there is nothing wrong with it either. If a person wants to do something their way and it only affects them, then so be it. Just because people know what they can work on does not mean that they will. To change, a person must want to. Just like becoming a SL and leading a prosperous life thereafter, you must have a desire to change like your life depends on it.

Think about the hungriest you have ever been. In fact, wake up in the morning, and don't eat for the next 15 hours. Do not plan this exercise, do it tomorrow. Continue your day as you would, but do not eat. At the end of the day, write down how you feel before you eat and what would you do for food. Not changing, not evolving into a SL, not prospering, should bring you these same feelings. As much as you crave food should be the same cravings you have to change and evolve. After you eat a healthy portion of your favorite meal, write down how you feel now. How excited you are that you accomplished this, how delicious the food was—it tasted better than ever. More than likely you are exhausted from the day, but look how excited you feel to have completed this evolution because of what it symbolized. These are the feelings a SL always have, they are continuously prosperous even in their [1]worst times, because they know and have experienced time after time that things will just keep getting better. SLs get the same side affects you acquired when being deprived from food (dizzy spells, low concentration, physically weak, etc.) when they are starved from progression. You must have a desire to change and evolve like you have one to eat to survive!

3. Know how to. So now you know you need to change and you have a real desire to, but you have no clue how. This is the most frustrating part by far, especially if you are not around the right resources to be of help. When you decide to grow

---

[1] Always remember, when things are at their very worst, you won't even know it.

and change Murphy's Law commences. Anything that can go wrong will. It is very demotivating. Progressing is like a plane taking off. When you are climbing altitudes to reach the desired level, your ears are popping, the plane is shaking, and you may experience some turbulence. However once you reach the desired altitude it becomes a smooth ride, until you climb again. The food experience can help you with this. First off, do not give up. Look for resources like you would look for a lost credit card or your car keys. There are more resources around you than you could ever imagine and honestly, most people want to help. All you have to do is ask. You never know who a person really is or what all they have accomplished in their life, no matter how good or bad a situation they are in. Simply *asking people for help* can frequently get you what you need or can send you in the right direction toward your request. Become actively receptive to opportunities, they are everywhere.

A great way to change, without thought, is to *manipulate yourself into doing positive things by turning it into a private competition*. Companies manipulate employees in a positive way. They give a sales goal, with the first person to reach it receiving a bonus of some sort. The military gives medals for different achievements. Or a sports MVP award goes to the person with the best statistics. All are built to increase competition and yield better results. Well when it comes to you as an individual, you set the bar. How high or low that bar is, is up to you. If you want to lose weight, start out by losing one pound this week. Next week try another one. Shoot for 5 pounds in a month, but give yourself some sort of competition with goals to work toward.

"If you don't go after what you want, you'll never have it.
If you don't ask, the answer will always be no.
If you do not step forward, you'll always get left behind."

Chapter 13

CHANGE DOES NOT HAPPEN OVERNIGHT

Do you have what it takes to really become a SL? Everyone has witnessed people rise to stardom or acquire large sums of money in what seems to be overnight. People then speculate that the fortunate person is "set for life;" even their children's children will be set for life off the infamous or rich person. However, what actually happens is that after all the fame and fortune, popular singers, athletes, or actors, become bankrupt, addicted to drugs, or fall to some other vice. This is because many people who become rich or famous in what seems to be overnight are not ready for what comes with it—and have never conquered adversity. Their reckless lifestyle does not have to be riddled with drugs and late nights, it can be the person who overworks and under appreciate themselves or their families. Some lottery winners blow through their winnings in no time at all, so it would do no good in most cases to just hand an "ordinary Joe" a million dollars. If you give a man a fish he eats for a day, if you teach a man to fish he eats for a lifetime. This is metaphorically the same with money. The get rich quick schemes and the fast money do no good. Become a skeptic when offers come your way that you know you have not earned. Anything you can get fast, you can lose fast; it is fool's gold.

If you have ever ventured into the woods and dug around as a kid, you may have found some fool's gold. Initially you think you have hit some kind of archaeological lottery because *perception is reality* and to a kid this mineral dug up surely resembles gold. Even as an adult you may think fool's gold is real until you scratch the surface and you see what it really is, fugazi. The public, the media, critics, your boss, your peers, it is the job of these people to scratch your surface. They want to be sure they have the real thing, real gold. The public is skeptical because throughout centuries they have been sold everything from snake oil to pyramid schemes, both fool's gold. Even worse, the public have followed leaders who are shams themselves.

It is all about your perception. There is no systematic way of preparing how to be rich and famous, but by knowing your identity you don't have to. Understanding who you are, admitting your faults, then changing yourself for the better is a fine-tuning process that must be done correctly if you are to ever become a successful leader. This process must be mastered because it is repetitive and it takes time. A SL is constantly changing and evolving for the better.

For example, shows like American Idol have the ability to expedite a singer's career. They come into the spotlight in a very short period of time, and their lifestyle changes drastically. The tours will cause them to be away from family, making a hotel their home, new people will be introduced into their life, some of whom they cannot trust or tell if they are there for them or their money, and the amount of money they receive and the new lifestyle they have will cause them to have to balance their budget differently. While all this is occurring, the singer must stay disciplined to their craft or the thing that got them into the spotlight will diminish. This means continuing to practice and rehearse and doing the things that keeps them relaxed and ready to perform no matter how long it takes. Many of the singers off American Idol become one hit wonders. Their ten minutes of fame is up before they know it because they were not ready to be in the position they were in. They got it fast, and then they lost it fast. If they were ready, they would have continued to flourish.

"You don't have to be 100 percent better by tomorrow, just get 1 percent better today and every day thereafter."

Chapter 14

UNDERSTAND LEADERSHIP AS AN ART

If you study—or even observe leaders, quickly you will realize leadership is an art. Just like art, leadership styles vary. There are leaders who rule out of fear, admiration, respect, or all three. Some micromanage with an iron fist, while others give everyone in the organization enough leeway to control their own fate. This art form is so profoundly significant because it literally changes history. History of people, families, and nations. To become a better SL you must study and practice this art form, just as you would any other. Observing and reflecting on past and present SLs. It is a class of its own kind.

Having people follow you may unintentionally make you a leader, but it does not mean you are competent. Look at the stages your followers are at in life and in their craft. This should be a good indicator of your competency as a leader. If your followers are constantly failing and not performing at a peak level, it is not them who are jacked up, it is you. A SL can take any group and flourish. Elite people, people who border being SLs themselves, enjoy being led by a person or group of people who not only have a strong purpose, but also know how to lead. A good leader gives people that well sought after security blanket in life. On the contrary, these same strong-willed, capable individuals will not allow themselves to perish figuratively or literally if they believe the person leading the charge is incompetent. Incompetence of a leader only has two outcomes eventually, no one follows, or worse mutiny abroad!!

One thing to always remember is just like leaders in the world, there are followers. It is just as much as an art to follow as it is to lead. Look at the vice president. While he certainly is a leader in his own right, his primary job is to follow and back up the president. The job title is made to follow. You learn how to become a great follower just as you would a leader. Observe and reflect on past and present SLs in that position. While mission success is often credited to the head honcho, these people always give all the credit to their team or the person under them, who was actually the most instrumental in accomplishing goals.

The same way a leader is created, is the same way a follower is created. There is absolutely nothing wrong with being a follower, especially when it benefits the whole organization. Chicago Bulls small forward, Scottie Pippen, played in what may seem like the shadow of Michael Jordan during their championship careers. Had Pippen gone to any other team, he would have not only continued to start, but would have also been the superstar. Yet Pippen continued to play for the Bulls where he was not the #1 player—in some eyes, but excelled with the organization and won a ton of championships.

There is a little bit of leader and follower in everyone, the question is how much. The important thing to know is which one you are and to play that role accordingly. For followers your thinking should shift from how you can complete your own mission, to completing the mission of the organization, which is established by the leader. A great follower, who is also a SL, will look for which organization has values that align to theirs and one that they would love to be a part of and work with. While ownership is preached, there is nothing wrong with working for someone. [1] If you know someone has a good plan, good company, good purpose, then put your time to use helping. 90 percent of all leaders would turn into some sort of follower overnight, if Bill Gates personally asked them to work under him. Why? The foundation he has established is one that aligns with many leaders purpose and because he is a great SL himself. You can still be an elite member of society working for someone. It is the idle work, the work with no purpose or passion, that doesn't allow you to reach your full potential.

"It's not what you do, it's how and why you do it."

---

[1] This will be seen in the submission chapter.

Chapter 15

THE 5 STAGES OF COMPETENCE

Similar to any skill set, levels of competence vary. There are said to be 5 stages of competence in a skill and the same stages are applicable to a SL. Many people make the mistake of thinking that an initial success means that they are really good at something. An egotistical flair of thinking you are better at something after a few weeks, than someone who has been doing it for years. This thought process is commonly revealed in professional sports when a rookie commences play and delivers mind-blowing performances. During their opening season some rookies shatter records while rewriting the way their position must be defended. However, more times than not, majority of these people do not reach the pinnacle of success that was ascribed to them. It is just another instance of fool's gold.

To become an elite leader, you must understand what stage you are at and the different stages there are to accomplish.

(1) Unconscious Incompetence-Know You Need To

This is the stage that many people perpetually live in. People are unaware that they are not good at something, instead they think they are doing alright. This is the worst and most dangerous stage to be in. This is the stage where initial success cause arrogant thinking of superiority and mastery, while in reality the person doesn't know the first thing about what they are doing. Sound familiar, fool's gold.

If you just started something, understand there are many areas of opportunity. There are experiences you have not had and fine details you have not yet learned to simply be the best. If you are not sure if you are in this stage or not, ask someone. Tell your close associates to be honest or ask a complete stranger for their opinion. This is a tough stage because people don't know any better. One way organizations have battled this is by outsourcing. Organizations will hire consulting firms who expertise in spotting the weak links. These consulting firms will come in, evaluate the organization from top to bottom, then tell the leadership why their stuff still stinks. They get paid very handsomely to do so because it works. Know you need to!

(2) Conscious Incompetence-Have A Desire

When a person reaches the stage of conscious incompetence they are making good progress. They realize that they are not good at whatever they are doing and become inspired to learn and get their hands on any resource that is going to get them to the next stage of conscious competence.

Here you learn that maybe your way of thinking, negative outlooks, or behavior have gotten you in the situation you don't want to be in. Instead of ignoring this problem and living in ignorance you decide to go out and change. You use any and all resources available. Reading, listening, and being mentored only by those who help change and motivate you for the better. In this stage you now see there are an abundance of resources at the tip of your fingers. You understand that people are here to help and it is possible for you to progress like you never imagined. The transition to this way of thinking is enlightening. Have a desire!

(3) Conscious Competence-Know How To

This is the stage where the seeds of a person's hard labor start to bear fruit. They may have spent weeks, months or years studying, learning and practicing their skills and finally have come to a stage where they are actually pretty good at what they do. They are far from being the best in their field, but they have some good authority and are a lot further than the majority of people who are still starting out. Now you know exactly how to get better. You have a good idea of what you need to do and how long it may take to reach the next step of your craft.

(4) Unconscious Competence

This is where you don't think about what you are doing and you still do it right. To those, who didn't see you come of age, will think your talents are innate. You can multitask and adapt to your surroundings with seamless effort. In reality, it is the harvest. You reap the seeds you sow. Your first seeds were planted when you initially began the journey of fixing the error in your ways. Now X time later, those seeds of smart work, persistence, and dedication, have sprouted and continue to flourish. When you are writing, your first thought is not "wow I'm writing with my right (or left) hand," you just write. Unconscious competence works the same way, you don't think about the task you are doing because it is second nature to you, but to others it may be a rare skill.

These four stages can be exemplified by driving a car. Initially you are at the stage of unconscious incompetence. You have sat next to people who drive you around for years and it seems so effortless and easy. You think it cannot be hard to drive, in fact you are pretty confident that if you get behind the wheel you could get from point A to B in one piece.

After attempting to get behind the wheel, you realize it is not so easy. All the moving parts of operating the vehicle seem overwhelming and the pressure applied to the gas and brake are never right. This is when you become aware of the fact that you actually suck at driving. You now pledge to take the necessary steps to become better. You are now at the stage of conscious incompetence.

After taking lessons, and lots of practice, you finally become better and stand ready to drive on the public road. Everything still feels a little uneasy and you focus on every action you perform while driving (accelerator, break, clutch, shift gears). You are now at the stage of conscious competence.

As you continue to drive and spend more time behind the wheel you begin to feel more comfortable with the action of driving. You start to focus less on things like shifting gears, accelerating, indicating and breaking because these actions have started to become a habit. You automatically do those things without thinking about it. This is the stage where you have good driving skills and you don't need to actively focus on the mechanical actions of your skills. You are now at the stage of unconscious competence.

After the fourth stage is grasped you can finally begin to hone in on becoming a master, if your [1]life circumstances allow. What the master does is CONSCIOUSLY considered every corner, and every parameter of every corner on the road, and gets constant immediate feedback on their practice performance. Then they do it consciously constantly, daily, for years. This takes many years, but day by day you can grow towards mastery.

---

[1] Some people intentionally choose not to become a master. If you perceive to begin your quest too late or it interferes with any other plans in life—usually time spent with family, then it is not uncommon for people to forfeit reaching the stage of mastery.

(5) Mastery

The mastery sequence is clear. So now you can drive unconsciously, navigate, talk on your cellular phone, and listen to the radio. However, you are still far from mastery. Chances are you can't remember how many times you changed gears on the way to work, or how many turns you took, let alone the approach and exit speeds on those turns. You do not yet have the necessary reaction ability, experience, and practice under the most difficult and dangerous circumstances, to be a true master. Masters are graceful under pressure. One popular rule of thumb, which has come about this century, is the 10,000 hour rule. This rule states that becoming a master in any craft requires you to put 10,000 hours of work into it. Some provisos to the rule include: the earlier you start practicing those hours the better and the person practicing must constantly strive to get better or they will plateau. You have to practice being successful and being a leader. Mastery can be explained by two historic figures with different rationales, but essentially the same meaning:

"Only one who devotes himself to a cause with his whole strength and soul can be a true master. For this reason mastery demands [2]all of a person."
-Albert Einstein-

"Excellence is an art won by training and habituation. We do not act rightly because we have virtue or

---

[2] Life circumstances would apply here.

excellence, but we rather have those because we have
acted rightly. We are what we repeatedly do.
Excellence, then, is not an act but a habit."
-Aristotle-

Constructive Criticism

Frequently when individuals reach top tier levels there are not many people left around who feel comfortable enough to speak candid to them. When you have been doing things right for so long it may be difficult for others to question your methods and you may even become unapproachable in critique. In the first instance, even if you are approachable, your record speaks for itself. Those around you know they might not understand the method to your madness, but because of continued prosperity they know and believe you have one. So it becomes difficult for them to know when to offer their advice in fear of trying to fix something that may not be broke. In the latter, a SL must know how to take constructive criticism. Remember there is always room for improvement. In life people will always criticize things you do. At times this criticism can seem demeaning or personal. Whether that is the case or not, listen to your critics and decipher what they are saying—not how they are saying it. If the information is actually helpful, then take heed and change your old ways. If it is not helpful, then say thanks and go about your methods as you would otherwise. Constantly have someone around who can and will be genuine with you at all times. Preferably someone who is not a subordinate to you. You must have the wherewithal to accept constructive criticism if you are to continuously mature. To achieve the level of mastery, *criticism is critical.*

> In everything you do, constantly consciously attempt it more effectively and efficiently.

There is a Lesson in Everything You Do

Always look at the mechanics of things. This is the mastery level you want to reach, where it becomes second nature to self-criticize. If you can easily identify how and why different situations work, you will always be in control if it is necessary. You will always be able to adapt and have the upper hand. Essentially you will create your own luck. Stock savvy investors who always make money in their picks (the Buffets if you will) are not lucky. These people speak of the countless amounts of hours they study their field to ascertain that area of expertise. The due diligence done by these investors is amazing. The amount of information you know about your favorite celebrity, television show, or athlete, is the same amount of information and time these investors spend learning about a company's profile. To the untrained eye they are lucky and just have a knack for picking the next thing to blow. In reality they are making very calculated decisions. Occasionally these people say they went with their [3]gut instinct. Subconsciously that gut reaction is actually the cognitive part of the brain adding past experiences and the statistical odds of an outcome. To them it feels like a gut instinct because it is second nature. When these people have reached their

---

[3] Prior Knowledge + Prior Experience = Gut Instinct.

72

legendary status they have scores of cognitive information to call upon in times when they must use that "gut decision" and show the world how "lucky" they are.

"Even if everyone tells you things you already know, you learn just how far ahead you are compared to everyone else."

Chapter 16

CHARACTERISTICS

These are the characteristics of SLs. Short, sweet, and to the point. If you realize you do not necessarily possess some of these characteristics, then working toward gaining them would be a positive course of action. All SLs have these traits intrinsically in some shape, form or fashion. Confidence runs parallel to every one of these characteristics. Confidence is something that is in everything. Confidence can enhance each characteristic and having these characteristics will improve your confidence.

Drive

Contrary to some beliefs, drive is innate. Many people are born with a carefree quit at will mindset, with either a low drive, or worse, no drive. Then there are the people born with the keep pushing never quit attitude. You wanting to do something cannot be taught or shaped by your environment. At the beginning of the day if you want to do something you decide to do it. *Drive* is your *will* to go. How fast you go or how hard you go is influenced by your passion. That is shaped by your purpose, environment, upbringing, peers, and so on. But to actually go is drive and it is up to you to decide to turn on the ignition.

To determine how much drive you have look at how much initiative you take. Initiative is taking action in the absence of instruction. When taking initiative you have to very proactive and resourceful. Things will either not get done or you will not get what you want, if you cannot go out and find creative ways to achieve your desired consequence. If you want a raise at work, a better grade in school, or a better position in your organization, then you need to take the initiative to make it happen. If you have a problem with something you have the option to do something about it or take it. It is that simple.

The creators of the first dotcoms, founders of some of the most recent technological companies (Microsoft, Oracle, Facebook, etc.) all have an incredible amount of drive. They all took the initiative upon themselves to start something new and unheard of and they all are being well paid for it.

Self-discipline

The only safeguard against human nature is self-discipline. Your moral compass can be strong, your standards high, and consistency synonymous with your name, but there will still be a tough time where human nature is tested. When this time occurs, you must have self-discipline. Drive and self-discipline are the overseers of your characteristics, without them you have nothing.

The chief aspect of self-discipline you must learn is arousal-control. Arousal-control is alluded to in the opening paragraph as the ability to tap into that reservoir of energy. You can become aroused when an excess amount of excitement takes over your mental capacity for thought. This is of the upmost importance because it's an innate part of human nature to have emotions and become aroused. It is the barbaric nature of people coming out. However, SLs always maintain their control and remain sensible. To think with a clear head you must be emotionally sound. All the high points as well as the low points in life, perceived through your thought processes, have the ability to tap into a person's emotional state. During this state people do not think clearly. There is extensive biological research on serotonin, testosterone, and adrenaline. Each chemical can either change a person's emotional state, level of aggression, and heart rate, respectively. It also adds a condition of sensory alertness, mobility, and a readiness to respond. So in high stress situations, positive or negative, your body will illicit an intense internal reaction. A SL will learn to not only recognize the onset of a high stress situation, but also the response from the body and know how to handle it.

Most people are not emotionally sound, which is why public relation firms and the folks in public affairs get paid so much. They are hired to write or announce messages and stances of an organization, or an individual, in a politically correct way. Similar to the consulting firms who spot the weak links in organizations, there are also consultants who train teams how to deal with emotional management, especially in the public. Everyone has once heard in their life to take a deep breath and count to ten when something goes wrong. This method is widely used because it gives your body time to get the oxygen and the slower heart rate needed to calm down. You think clearer when this happens. Having the knowledge to recognize the onset of an emotional high/low and then being able to counteract the negative impact is crucial to becoming emotionally sound. It is known as being professional. When athletes lose big games, the reporters are at times just as fierce as the opponent was. Still the athlete has to stay professional and positive, maintain a cool head, and answer the questions. If they are angry about the lost, as they should be, the interview is not the time to display that anger. A SL will explain their anger, not display it. Reserve your emotions for only those worthy of them.

A post loss example, Non SL Athlete: How do you think I feel?!? This is crap we lost. The referees cheated, my teammates messed up, and the coach called the wrong plays. I don't like being here anymore and I don't have anything else to say!! That was the PG version, but you get the picture. SL Athlete: We worked hard all week for the game, while we are upset that we lost the other team played well. All we can do now is go back to practice and continue to get better. An emotionally sound SL is able to control their feelings and keep a clear mind, so personal biased decisions will not affect everyone and potentially cost themselves a job.

Impulse is the assassin of discipline. Once you have your emotions intact you can begin to get yourself intact. Re-wire your mind to have conscious control of your body. Sticking to promises you made to others and yourself takes self-discipline.

Not going to hang out late when you have something important to do the next day takes self-discipline. Many things that seem like good decisions at the moment are just impulses. It is you turning away from discipline and turning toward your innate behavior. Going out or spending time and money before budgeting your life and bills is just as barbaric as a dog chasing a cat. Do what is right, not what feels right. Be rational, not visceral.

The uncontrollable illicit reactions, these impulses, are nothing more than arousals. Here are the steps to practice better arousal-control:

1. Take a step back and evaluate—give yourself a break.
2. Find a trusted place to vent—that place of peace.
3. Do not linger on the problem.
4. Realize you are not the first and you will not be the last person to face this.
5. Process your emotions.
6. Realize the situation can be a lot worse—perception is reality.
7. Acknowledge your thoughts.
8. Uncover what you are really aroused about.
9. See this as an opportunity to better yourself or the process.
10. Analyze the situation, focus on actionable steps.
11. Identify how it occurred, so it won't occur again next time.
12. Pick out the learning points from the encounter.

Integrity

When there is an abundance of peer pressure to do the wrong thing, sociological studies have shown that people often will. The bystander effect, also called the Genovese syndrome, is a psychological phenomenon that refers to cases where individuals do not offer any means of help in an emergency situation to the victim when other people are present. Popular reasons for this is because people are supposedly less likely to view the situation as a problem and will less likely take the responsibility to assume action. Not to say for good reason, bystanders have families, careers, and their own lives to worry about. Nevertheless, at the end of the day it boils down to courage. The truth of the matter is that there is not an abundance of people that *have the courage to take action.*

Think about the people who fight back. The everyday citizens with "average" jobs, who are rarely placed in situations where their fight or flee response kicks in and they choose to fight. Attacking a terrorist on a plane, unions, or the Charles Ramsey's of the world. Courage is also seen in instances such as the 2012 Aurora movie theater shooting, by those who covered their loved ones. Or in Sandy Hook, where teachers calmed students as the situation unfolded. All these people are considered fearless heroes. These people are not fearless, they are not adrenaline junkies, these people are courageous. They have their moral compass in place and know the difference between right and wrong. Depending on the extremity of the circumstance, *courageous people will step up.* Courage in the average everyday sense is used morally. When something is going against a person's values/morals in an extreme situation, they will gather the inner strength to stand up, no matter how severe the consequences. When exercising integrity you will often need to have a lot of courage. Especially in the workplace when you know something is inherently wrong, but standing up may turn you into a pariah and in some cases get you fired. No job is worth risking your integrity. Integrity takes courage.

What else influences integrity? Judgment. This involves being able to think about things clearly and calmly, and then making an unbiased decision that yields the most 3E results. The decisions you make not only affect you, but as a SL, the decision usually affects those around you. When you make poor decisions you must also have the courage and integrity to take responsibility. Everyone has had an occasion where they have done the wrong thing or made a slew of wrong choices, but you knew you must come forward with the truth. No matter how deep of a hole you have dug yourself into, the truth will set you free. People will at the least know they can trust you to come forward with honesty when there are tough decisions to be made.

The last and perhaps the most important trait of integrity is character. Your character is as it sounds, a character. It is what everyone external to yourself see you as. You shape your own character, no one else, no matter what the situation. You are shaping your character every day, every minute, your whole life. Your character is one of the few things you are truly in control of. If a movie fanatic sees an actor play a gang banging murderer in ten movies, and then on his eleventh role he plays a priest, the priest role would be hard to believe. The actor may evoke an ill feeling in some audience members because viewers are so used to seeing the actor as a killer. This is how actors become type casted. A large part of integrity comes from the character you are in the real world. Your integrity is not something that can be bought or bartered with. Know who you want to be in society, have clear morals and values and stick by them. You will be type casted in the real world. Know who your character is.

Your word is your bond. It is worth more than any handshake and it should be equal to a legal contract. If you say you are going to do something then do it. In the fast pace world of today trust seems like it is hard to build, but it is not. It is as simple as keeping your word. If people see they can trust you with little things, like you following up on a promise—whether it is fulfilled or not—then they will become more apt to trust you with bigger issues and projects. On the flipside, you not keeping your word is a major character flaw in any organization and your position there will not last long. Even in the underworld of criminals, lying is not accepted and neither is not doing what you said. There is no where you can go with low levels of integrity and be trusted. No one anywhere appreciates this. Low levels of trust increase the cost of business. Low levels of trust mean that someone must constantly check over you and your work, thus losing man hours in other areas and increasing the time of doing business. No one, anywhere, will ever want to pay more and spend more time on something, they can get cheaper, better, and faster. Integrity is doing what you say, saying what you mean, and meaning what you say. It is putting sound moral principles and honesty above all else. Traits that influence your integrity are courage, judgment, and character. It is only through value-based behavior that one is empowered to build trusting and lasting relationships that lead to individual and team success. Everything you do sets precedence as to who you are and what you will tolerate.

Vision

Your vision needs to be realistic to you or no one else will believe it. People have some of the most unique visions about where they want to take themselves, their families, and their companies one day, and those who inherently believe in it, and work toward it, accomplish it. Your vision is where you see yourself in the future. Some people call it dreaming, but it is not. A dream is something you unconsciously conjure up. No real expectations or consequences for that matter. A dream is your small slice of heaven, but with no outline to get there. A vision has some conscious effort and thought put into it. "I will get here in ten years, by doing these things, and by …" That is a vision. The first people into outer space may have dreamed about the experience there, but it was their vision that made the parts of the process start to move and become a reality. The problem with dreams is that people are too busy sleeping instead of pursuing them.

Vision, like drive, will help determine your value in the marketplace and your true earning potential. When Target first opened if their vision was to only have one department store in Minnesota, their earning potential would be severely crippled.

They would have limited themselves to one specific audience. However, the vision was to have Target's everywhere throughout the United States (now even expanding to Canada), thus making *the idea* of a Target that much more valuable.

Anticipation is a skill that can make or break any person or company, and it is something visionaries are good at doing. When sharing your vision with your organization, it is important to share not only the keys to success, but also potential roadblocks.

Those unexpressed needs in the Ritz-Carlton's mission statement are a form of anticipation. Fast food chains demonstrate anticipation by adding playpen areas for kids. These chains anticipate more children will want to come and stay if there is a play area. They know kids are not paying, so why provide this [1]complementary service? In most cases parents will go to restaurants where their children can eat and have a fun experience all at one place. Restaurants know this and bank on it. Take note, *leaders anticipate*.

Ray Lewis, a future Hall of Famer, was a professional linebacker in the National Football League for 17 years. That is a long time to be in the NFL period, but especially at that position. It is an even longer amount of time to be consistently successful. In the past when Lewis was asked how he stayed on

---

[1] Nothing in life is free or easy. There is not anything that is free, has been free, or will ever be free so stay vigilant when things are offered as such. You pay for everything somehow. If a sports star walks into a bar and gets a complimentary drink, it is complementary not free. They paid for the drink with their hard work in the game and their character and behavior outside of the game. All payments do not have to be monetary.

top of his game, he attributed it to studying game film. Lewis watched film on specific players of the opposition, opposing teams, his team, and maybe the most, of himself. Lewis looked for patterns, habits, clues, and cues, on all the film he studied. When it was time to play, the fine little details and ticks, which Lewis saw from opposing players, allowed him to anticipate what would happen next. This allowed Lewis to get to the spot where the ball was before anyone else, not just because of his athleticism, but because Lewis anticipated what would happen next and acted, not reacted.

Take a step back and see the big picture. Observe. After doing this enough times in life you will soon see that many situations repeat themselves, just as history often does. By knowing what triggers certain situations, you will become more apt to identify and act, consequently causing a more favorable outcome when they occur. Vision and anticipation adds that mystique to you that get people on the bandwagon. If you can anticipate something happening before it does, then use that anticipation to create favorable results, it will enhance you as a SL.

The masses are only concerned with their own welfare; this is why they are what they are and not SLs. The masses see the present, SLs see the future. In your business, no matter what the craft, you must have divine-like vision. Millionaires become the people to dominate industries, while billionaires are the revolutionaries who transform and spawn new ones. Visionaries have to be confident to believe in their own vision.

A textbook revolutionary, with divine-like vision, is seen in none other than Henry Ford. A true innovator, Henry Ford figured out what people wanted before they even knew they wanted it. Henry Ford is attributed to the quote:

> "If I asked the customer what they wanted, they would've said a faster horse."

Intelligence

People do not like being led by an incompetent person. Money cannot buy you respect, nor does power. No matter how high the pay of your subordinates or how much power you possess over them, respect will not be given unless you have proved you are well beyond fit for the job. No one likes their time wasted and as a SL it is a part of your duty to know what you are talking about and what you are doing in your domain. Whatever it is you do for a living or even for fun, you should at least have a basic knowledge of it, as well as the policies that go along with it.

You can raise your level of competence and intelligence by simply seeking knowledge. Any functioning human being has the ability to become formally educated. It is the application of education and informal knowledge (common sense) that builds your perception of intelligence. A good speaker and presenter can be perceived as very intelligent by the public because it is considered a rare skill. Public speaking does hold a high rank among people's fears. Although to a group of public speakers that may not be the same way they weigh intelligence, because to them they all are capable of doing it well. Therefore intelligence is only a perception that is interchangeable in different circles.

Some people have earlier experiences that help build their common sense. Your perception of intelligence and formal education can be severely offset if you have common sense and you can use context clues to figure things out. Not only learning about the world around you, but also being able to present new information to people who might have not been exposed to the same experiences as you (as illustrated in chapter seven).

There are people in this world that will travel just to try different meals and record the recipe. Imagine a man who does this. He never actually cooks, nor does he have any formal education in the culinary arts. Just a well-traveled person, who loves to eat. On his travels he records famous recipes in a journal, so when he returns home, someone can cook it for him. As he travels, the man always gives out a few recipes for people to try, they do, and they love it. The man is regarded as being one of the most knowledgeable chefs to some because of the recipes he introduces to people in various parts of the world. The man is not trying to gain notoriety in a dishonest fashion, but he travels so often and eats so much, the recipes he gathers are considered common knowledge to him. Well as the new saying goes, common sense is so rare it should be classified as a superpower. You never know what information others have or have not gathered. The more information you gather from exposure, travel, books, etc. and share, will greatly increase your perceived intelligence and competence, helping you to become a better SL.

Responsible

A SL must be responsible. A SL is the last line of defense for every organization that possesses one. No matter how tough things are or how great things are going, being responsible means that you will not be relaxed in your work ethic.

There are a few things that define a person as responsible. Initially it is being reliable. Being reliable is a primary duty for a SL. It means you can be relied upon to properly perform duties, you can be trusted with assignments—both formal and informal, and you consistently put forth your best effort—parallel to high standard levels. Reliability is a lot like character. Once you are labeled as reliable or not it sticks. Like character it is constantly being tested and SLs constantly rise up to the occasion with passion to show they are who they are. Informally, it matters. If you tell a friend or teammate you will do something or be somewhere at a given time, follow through. That person will know they can depend on you and you will more likely become the first person they think of when something positive arises. This translates the same in the workplace in a more formal fashion. A SL is always at work on time—or communicates otherwise, completes assignments on time, and their word is their bond, just as a signed contract. When you are labeled as reliable in the workplace, new opportunities will increasingly manifest, subsequently making "job security," that much more secure.

The next thing that defines a person as responsible is being results oriented. Finishing the job and finishing it in a 3E manner. In ancient kingdoms the messenger of bad news would be punished by having their head cut off, thus erecting the phrase—

don't kill the messenger. Today, while not as barbaric, the messenger still takes negative feedback for bringing bad news. To organizations that are high functioning, with high standards, and expect nothing but the best, bad news is seen as excuses. Whether directly (making the actual excuse of why you did not perform) or indirectly (actually delivering a message), excuses are not results oriented, responsible, nor does it display a trait of a SL. SLs bring back results, not excuses. If results cannot be achieved, SLs bring back solutions with problems. If you cannot bring back the solution everyone was looking for, do not come back empty handed. Solutions can come in the form of recommendations, alternatives and action steps to take, to get the results.

This highlights the fact that becoming a SL is a work in progress. Even if you are not currently an executive of a major company, a business owner, a captain of a sports team, or possess any type of major role in any organization, you can benefit from this guide. Every time there is a problem, there is another chance to raise your stock as an individual. Even if there is not a "problem" per say, there might be a more 3E way in a process that is waiting for you to discover. This is where your drive and initiative must kick in. Be the person who brings something back, don't present problems as being infinite. Solve enough problems and you will start to be look upon as the go to person. This gives you the stage and audience you need to take more initiative and show the organization why you are a SL and eventually, your vision.

Finally, nothing says responsible like a sense of ownership. United States Marines are infamous for their strict discipline and order that their leadership demands. One Gunnery Sergeant teaches ownership in the following way:

> "Once a decision is made and the order is given to execute it, carry out that order willingly as if it were your own, no matter how good or bad it is. While it may be the easy option to point the finger when the order is not directly yours, it actually works against you. Those who are your peers or subordinates do not see you as a leader in the light anymore, but more equal and you lose power and authority. If you are not the right person for the job then this may actually be a good thing. By taking ownership no matter how good or bad a decision is, it comes across as being yours, as it should."

This does not just go for orders. Have ownership in everything you do. If you make a mistake, take ownership of it. If a team member makes a mistake on a project you are heading take ownership! Throwing someone under the bus will not keep you off the hot seat for long because now your skills as a leader come under fire. It is always better to just report the mistake, what went wrong, the steps you have ALREADY put in place to fix it, and why it will never happen again. As a SL, taking ownership means that you are directly responsible for everything and everyone under or around you. If you are in charge of a project—no matter how insignificant it may seem—take ownership of it. You could be given an assignment that may seem frivolous to you, but it could mean the world to your superior. Or perhaps even, it is just a test to see how you treat the little things, because in most cases if you blow off the little things, there will be a day when you do it to the bigger things that matter. You can only gain greater responsibilities after you handle small ones and show people you are competent enough to get things done. You are your own worst enemy. No one else can control the choices you make, no excuses. That is what being responsible teaches. You have to hold yourself accountable for your actions before you worry about anyone else doing it for you.

The Blue Angels is the United States flight demonstration squadron. The pilots fly F/A-18 Hornets (jets) in tight formations performing maneuvers reaching speeds up to 700 mph at some estimated 10 inches of separation. You have to be extremely skilled to become a member of this squadron. What is more interesting about this squadron though is the pilots and how they critique themselves. In training and after flights they meet in a room and each member writes down on their own sheet of paper what they did wrong. They don't expect for someone else to correct them, they want their teammates to know they also recognized the mistake and is taking the appropriate course of action to correct it. To spectators, nothing they do could be perceived as wrong. A great show with no crashes is how an onlooker can judge. The pilots though, who fly these jets so close to each other and constantly practice performances, can tell if their teammate was an inch off the mark or a second late however. The pilots writing down their own mistakes and then sharing those mistakes with the rest of the team, builds trust. Teammates know everyone takes ownership and is accountable for everything they do. When you are flying that fast and that close to each other, you must trust your teammate and taking ownership increases that trust.

Mental toughness

When the chips are down and the odds are against you, how will you react? [2]Mental toughness is having a psychological edge that enables you to be consistent, confident, focused, and determined during high pressure situations in order to perform at maximum potential. SLs that are mentally tough not only show up in stressful situations, but they excel. In athletics, many personal records are often set after a significant or traumatic event in the athlete's life. Instead of sitting the game out, the athlete usually chooses to play and directs all of their negative energy from the event, to energy expended in their contest, the outcome is usually an incredible game on their part.

The below article published by the Associated Press (December 22, 2003) suitably illustrates mental toughness:

OAKLAND, Calif. (AP) -- On the night his father died, Brett Favre addressed the Green Bay Packers in an emotional team meeting. He said he had no intention of leaving his football family, even at one of the lowest points in his life.

---

[2] As defined by Ralph Jean-Paul.

The next day, Favre played his heavy heart out, inspiring his teammates to do great things.

Favre passed for 399 yards and four touchdowns a day after his father's death, moving into second place in NFL history for career TD passes while leading the Packers to a 41-7 victory over the Oakland Raiders on Monday night.

"I knew that my dad would have wanted me to play," Favre said. "I love him so much, and I love this game. It's meant a great deal to me, to my dad, to my family, and I didn't expect this kind of performance. But I know he was watching tonight."

With a series of spectacular long passes that somehow found his energized teammates, Favre decimated the Raiders' patchwork defense with one of the greatest performances in his 13-year career. He finished just 3 yards shy of his career high while sending the Raiders to their worst loss in eight years.

Favre threw for a personal-best 311 yards and four TDs in the first half, quickly turning a crucial game for the Packers' playoff hopes into a blowout victory.

Favre, who went 22-of-30, smiled and hugged his teammates throughout the game. On the sideline in the fourth quarter, he embraced wife Deanna before they headed home to Mississippi.

"What he had to deal with today was immeasurable," receiver Antonio Freeman said. "You can't put a price on what he did tonight. I don't know how he did it, but he did it in fine fashion."

Irvin Favre died of a heart attack Sunday night while driving near his son's hometown of Kiln, Miss. Brett decided to stay with the Packers (9-6) long enough to lead a victory that kept them in a tie with Minnesota atop the NFC North.

"I do not wish this on anyone," Favre said. "My dad has been to every game from fifth grade, and he coached me in high school. You never expect it to happen like that. I'm going to miss him. He was so instrumental not only in football, but in life."

Mental toughness is a quality that people usually learn indirectly from their experiences. Despite what many think, there are a variety of ways to consciously build mental toughness. You can begin to build mental toughness by simply using passion as propulsion for whatever it is you are trying to accomplish. Take ownership of your objective. Make that personal competition with yourself of why this objective is important. Think of your purpose in life and how this objective relates to it. Your purpose is the reason why you wake up and go every day, so this should be motivation in its own right. Understand that if you don't complete the objective at hand, it will stifle your progress toward your purpose and possibly your own livelihood. Think of those who depend on you to succeed for their own wellbeing, a family member, a friend, or a close associate. In any competition the person who is willing to lay it all on the line will win. If you are a businessman or in school that means you will work the extra hours, go without sleep, and close your blinds to the world until the objective is complete. If it involves you doing something physically this means, no matter how tired you are, how much pain you are in, you will continue to push.

When objectives are taken personally people have an extra edge. Take the war in the Middle East for example. [3]Many of the fighters there have an objective to push the U.S. out of their country, their home. In the last few years the U.S. has changed the strategic stance and military doctrine of how the war in the Middle East will be fought. Essentially it has become a war on the hearts and minds of the local population. The perception of the U.S. in the Middle East must be changed to those residents, if a real win is to occur, otherwise they will to continue to fight, until no one is left. If an assailant came into your home and threatened you and your family, the intensity in which you would fight back would be dramatically different in comparison to a weekend bar brawl. Passion will place the fire, not only in your belly, but also in your mind. The more you care, the more you continue to get back up and fight, no matter how many times you fail, you will continue to become mentally tough.

You are working on a limited timeline, your first two attempts have already failed, superiors, subordinates, peers, and your own psyche are all losing faith in your ability for favorable results. This causes you to become nervous, question your methods, and even yourself as the one to take this project on. These are the situations that cause people to tap out, quit, or

---

[3] Doesn't matter if their cause is right or wrong, concentrate on the edge.

make excuses. These are the adverse situations where you must move forward. Continue to do what you do. Not necessarily use the same method, but to take charge of the situation and figure out the solution, none the less passion. Continue to speak and carry yourself with complete confidence. Sometimes the level of greatness you seek lies just beyond the point you have convinced yourself your idea will not work.

This next way to build mental toughness is persistence. It allows you to bounce back quickly after setbacks, produce results even when the likelihood of success is low, and be unshakeable through any circumstance. Turn your mind and body on autopilot when it comes to goal completion. Robotic. Knowing nothing or no one will stop you from what you have your sights on. It doesn't matter if they tell you, you aren't: smart enough, big enough, fast enough, too many people in the position, too many applications already, not enough time, NO! A great example of persistence can be embodied by NFL cornerbacks.

A cornerback's primary job is to defend the receiver. Stop the offensive player (opposite person) from catching the ball. Receivers catch balls *all* the time. Passing and catching is one of the biggest parts of football and integral to the success of an offense. However time after time no matter how many catches or touchdowns a receiver gets on a given day, a good corner will not stop playing their game. Smart, assertive, patient, and persistent. Until "BOOM!" Interception. An interception occurs when a corner "takes" a ball from a receiver. This is done after a pass has been thrown (after the ball is thrown) and in the air toward the receiver. While the ball is directed to the receiver, it is not his. He is not in ownership of the ball. Whoever wants it, usually who wants it more (passion) gets it. Interceptions are not given though. You must be a corner in life. Persistently aiming to "take" everything, but rejection—the no (within legal and ethical bounds). A corner is allowed to do just about anything to get their interception except touch the other player.

Parallel this to your life. You can take any position you want, don't worry about the competition. Their reputation, intelligence, or connections are all none of your concern. Respect your opponent. Don't walk into a job interview and not know anything about the company or the person who is interviewing you. Don't walk into your boss's office or a meeting either without knowing all the ends and outs of information; this is a quick way to lose credibility. Due diligence is respect, and you must have that. However, *you* can only control *you* and in structural instances the world around you. You must be able to do what you can, with what you have, where you are. Persistence will allow you to withstand pain, fatigue, stress, and hardship. Just know,[4]"It's hard to beat someone who never quits."

People are taught to be enthusiastic and confident but aren't taught bravado. Bravado is having the willingness to lose, be proved wrong or fail, and still decide to go on and try for something attainable. Bravado means when you are given an opportunity to showcase something you work toward, you do it and do it with conviction.

---

[4] Babe Ruth.

It takes a lot of bravado to face adversity time and time again. Adversity is a fistfight. In this fight you don't have to win, but will you at least fight? Attack adversity the same way you would your freedom. People didn't and don't become free because they want it really bad and they hope it comes, but will not stand and face an oppressor. Freedom comes when you don't accept anything else but it, you continue to fight for it, and you never lower your standards on your definition of it. There is no compromise with freedom, and neither is it with adversity. If you are in a corner, if all odds are stacked against you, tucking your tail is not a rational option. Giving up is not ok, if you are going to lose or go down, do it on your own terms, not on anyone else's. When you see an adverse situation form, go after it. Stand tall no matter what the situation is and attack it. At the very least, you will have your own self-respect and confidence intact and everyone else will always respect you for it. Are you free right now? Are you: mentally, emotionally, physically, and financially, free?

The Apollo Theater is a famous auditorium in Harlem, New York. It has been the proving grounds for comedians, singers, and other entertainers alike for decades. Here if you do not have bravado, you will undoubtedly fail. Dave Chappelle spoke before about being booed at the Apollo when he was performing as an adolescent teen. After being booed, Chappelle got kicked off the stage by the sandman. The "sandman" is like a rodeo clown for the Apollo. When entertainers have been booed enough and the crowd feedback is so negative, the sandman is sent out on stage to shoo the entertainer away. The sandman then proceeds to tell a couple of jokes and maybe a quick comedic dance to get the crowd back into a joyful spirit. Dave said that time at the Apollo was the "best experience" he has had because he "failed so miserably." Chappelle said the experience "was not that bad," the failure gave him bravado. Chappelle said he knew that there was "nothing else in the entertainment realm that could make him feel that humiliated," so since he faced it and survived, he became "fearless." This is a climatic transformation of Chappelle as a comedian, after this experience he became mentally and emotionally free to perform. You must keep raising the bar, until the day comes you meet your match, and win or lose, your threshold will reset to a level like none other before and you too, will not only have some bravado in the way you carry yourself, but you will become fearless.

The final way to consciously build mental toughness is to conquer adversity, whenever you face it. Adversity is one of the four facets that show a person's true character. The others being wealth, success, and failure. When people are facing an adverse situation everything that embodies them is put on the forefront. Some of those who seem strong begin to crumble, drop the ball, or selfish, (intentionally or not) producing an undesired effect on the group. Others are capable of the exact opposite. There are people, intentionally or not, that will rise in these situations. Occasionally it is the person everyone least expects, who unexpectedly flips the switch and begins to produce momentous results.

The essence of adversity is the situation associated with it. As the situation transpires it begins to mold you as a person. Failure can be an outcome of an adverse situation, but adversity itself is a character building event. It cuts an individual into a leader and on the structural level it becomes a critical time for an organizations growth, as well as setting precedence for the culture and climate. Adversity is nothing more than a minor setback. Setbacks turn to opportunities, and SLs make them challenges. Keep in mind these five things during adverse times.

Setback→Opportunity→Challenge

1. Negative thinking leads to withdrawal.
   - Do not use your flight response, now is the time to fight!
2. Identify with what you want.
   - Remember why you are here. In this situation what did you hope to accomplish? Use the same expectation management as you would when you and your organization consider the parameters of failing.
3. Don't disengage, reduce occurrences.
   - Passion breeds persistence. When something matters enough there is no such thing as giving up or taking no for an answer. Passion breeds sincere optimism and a willingness to accept a challenge. Never give up, never surrender! Keep at it; just be conscientious about the mistakes you make.

4. Disconnect.
   - When it is time to turn the "off" switch on the setback, do so. Do not let a setback consume you and tear you apart from the inside out.
5. Moving.
   - The hardest part of anything is moving. Do not freeze up. Setbacks will happen and that is when adversity kicks in. As a SL your team cannot afford for you not to make a decision. Freezing up is purely selfish. Hesitation to lead will cause other people or organizations to take the authoritative role and once this occurs rarely is it given back. Make a decision and move forward with confidence.

Adaptability

The ability to adapt is an important characteristic in any SLs arsenal. Sometimes life is chaotic. Even the best planners and strategist cannot account for every variable in different situations, so to ensure results in the end, one must be able to adapt to those unseen variables. Whether you are understaffed, underfunded, or out of time, remember SLs bring back results. Adaptability is a characteristic that is a make or break for a SL. There are the valuable players who only deliver in their comfort zone and then there are those who always deliver regardless of the situation. These people are known as invaluable, SLs. It is relatively easy to develop this characteristic. Instead of doing the same routine all the time shake up your life and add some spontaneity. When you are thrown a curve ball, when it matters most, you will more likely be able to stay confident outside of your comfort zone and get the job done.

Adapting to people requires tact. Tact means you can deal with people in a manner that will maintain good relations and avoid unnecessary conflict. In a professional sense, just be respectful, but firm in your business. In formal settings, you are not there to make friends; your likeability will never supersede results. SLs can succeed with anyone; the primary reason is that it benefits the organization as well as their goals. It doesn't matter if you are paired with a new boss, subordinate, or peer the biggest day of your career, SLs will find common ground and get the work done. Being adversarial will get you nowhere. Tact and diplomacy are essential to survival.

Adapting to the environment involves using decisiveness. This means making good decisions without delay. Remain calm, get all the facts, and work quickly to make a sound decision. The worst decision a leader can make is not making one at all. You will not get or stay in any position of leadership if you cannot make a decision. It is always difficult to make the best decision under pressure, especially when ethical issues are at stake. This is why you must know who you are. In these instances you trust your training and thought processes as a person, then decide. Never relax, but always remain calm.

Teamwork

Whether you are looked on as a superior, subordinate, or as a peer, you are a part of a team. Not only must you be able to carry your own weight, but you must know how to trust others to do the same. A SL is devoted to their team. They are selfless and unselfish, never using their position or rank for personal gain, at the expense of others. Thought processes and decisions of a SL are always and only made with *the team being in mind*. When you take care of your team, when their needs are met and their wants are attainable, their whole focus transfers over to the mission and to the leader responsible. Their effort level exponentially increases because they believe in what they are doing and who they are doing it for. Give your team the task at hand and watch how expediently they work toward it, never giving a second thought about any worries. Your job is ensuring they have all the tools at their disposal to get the job done and giving credit when it is deserved. Not just the internal tools at work such as the right equipment and training, but external tools for their personal needs. Time off for family, time off for relaxation, money for expenses, visual perception of upward mobility in the organization, upward mobility in and of the organization itself, security, etc. When these factors are met, when the SL goes above and beyond to ensure the team is comfortable enough to just concentrate on work, the team will go above and beyond to ensure the mission is complete. If this becomes the work climate, where everyone is well taken care of and there are [5]good people on the team, the organization cannot fail. Goals of the team cannot be accomplished alone, nor are they meant to be. Take pride in knowing you can trust those you work with.

Your commitment and loyalty to the team is of the upmost importance and these are the things that will continuously be tested. Commitment to the team involves ensuring everyone is not only performing to the standard, but well above it, and then continuing to reach for new levels to reset the bar. If you start a company today and the minimum for entry-level employees is to have a college degree, ten years from now that minimum should be a college degree and experience, or depending on the acceleration of the company, possibly a masters. Team commitment is also focused around trust. Not just trust that the team will get the job done, but trust in their methods. Trust in the ideas they run up the ladder and chain of command. Good ideas come from your team and you want the people you work with to be comfortable enough to bring them to the forefront, if it will help the team. The team's commitment to growth is equally significant. Yearly redundancy does not breed a conducive environment for more SLs. If you want your team to succeed, you have to keep pushing beyond what you think you can do and find out what you're really capable of.

Loyalty to the team revolves around devotion. Devotion to your seniors, peers, and subordinates. Mistakes and failures will occur. Depending on your position and your team some of these

---

[5] Good-people with the same or similar values as a SL. They take pride in their work, doing it with a higher purpose and will not compromise their integrity. They care for and look after those around them.

will become public. Public doesn't always mean the general public. Public can translate to an internal affair. The internal affair could possibly be another department at your company, the different levels of positions at your company, or a rival organization. Regardless of who it is, always remember your loyalty. You never discuss your problems of your team with outsiders and you never talk unfavorably about those senior in front of your subordinates. Doing this will not only make the team look bad, and vulnerable, but it will also make you look unfavorable. The thinking from another person will shift from the team, to what you are doing to make it better or worse. Look at some of the United States prosperous organizations. Some of these include: Google, Apple, The CIA, The Navy SEALs, Microsoft, the Patriots; there is an extensive list. These are all more alike than you think. All of these organizations share common ground in SLs behavior. Every one of these organizations brings the right people in and when these people decide to leave, they leave sharper than ever. One very similar thing they all have and practice is their *code of silence*. Secrecy. Their internal matters, for the most part, stay internal. This established climate is rarely attainable, though not unachievable. Their *secrets to success* are not shared with the public, even though their secret ingredient is right under your nose. *Silence.*

The climate is the overall feel and characteristics of an organization. A good work climate at a minimum includes: professionalism, trust, hardworkers, discipline, and reliability, just to name a few. Conversely the climate can be deteriorated with one of these destructive things such as: distrust, apathy, laziness, unreliability, no/low self-control, etc. Everyone should take ownership in improving and maintaining the climate, but it is ultimately the SL who is directly responsible for it. Everyone looks up to you and knows you are the go to person in tight situations; you have become synonymous to what your organization is and what it represents. You are an ambassador everywhere you go for your community, so your actions and words determine how everyone else will carry the reputation of said community as well. By doing the right thing at all times and becoming that beacon of light everyone can look toward for direction, you can and will dictate the climate. The climate will determine how big and how prosperous your organization will grow to be. Before the death of Steve Jobs, president/CEO of Apple, he built a climate of innovation. Steve Jobs made it for those not only in his own company, but in the technology community itself, to feel ok with designing something totally different, and absurdly unconventional. Now that same climate Jobs help build is broader than ever, spanning across companies worldwide, with the idea that doing something unconventional, while it has its risk, can also become a home run. How is the climate in your life? What is your personal climate about yourself, are you happy? How is it at work, school, in your organization, in your family? Here is your chance to change and/or improve that climate.

You could be selfish and become perceived as the best man, but what a team needs is more great SLs. The wealthy flourish in environments of collaboration and cooperation. The "rich" and the underclass contend in the environments of independence. Your team is more apt to succeed and to have continued success if everyone works with each other. Liking one another is optional, but respecting another individual's talents and maintaining a high level of professionalism is a must for ascension and prosperity. Metaphorically, the team is a fist. Four fingers and a thumb are weak individually however together they form a fist. A fist is a weapon, and depending on how well you can manipulate the fist determines how lethal it is. A group of people, a team, becomes a fist. Depending on how well you all work together and mesh, will determine how successful you will be. Your aim, no matter what your position in an organization, should be one of synergy. Find people who you would go out of your way for so they can do the same for you. References to "the circle" are well known. In a tight-knit group people are referred to either being in or out the circle. The circle's significance is that it represents synergy. Everything inside the circle must function in sync. As a SL people should be able to come to you and express themselves in a judgment free zone and receive feedback in a positive form even if it is critical. In good and bad times, be open-minded, understanding, and provide support.

When professional sport teams go to the championship game, they will bring everyone. Literally everyone involved in their teams success. The starting players, the bench players, the injured players, trainers, interns, close friends of the organization, managers, and even the custodians' get tickets. Everyone. Some of it is superstition. If a certain person has been there since day one when you started to win, then there is no reason to leave them behind now and risk the bad luck. That's just some of it, a very little piece. The real reason no one gets left behind is because everyone played some part in getting the team to the championship. Even the custodians who scored some tickets are important to the team and are treated with just as much respect as a player. If the facilities are not clean and up-kept, then that becomes one more distraction taking the rest of everyone else's attention off of their job. In successful organizations, everyone will get to know their role and position. While it is always good to become knowledgeable about other positions, you must trust that the person there knows what they are doing. In turn, stay in your lane and become a subject matter expert on the things you are good at. If you are a SL in a position of power, make the right calls, if you are a SL in a subordinate position, do your job. The goal is more important than the role. Have a total understanding of the value of teamwork and the positive impact that each individual has on results produced by the team.

Charismatic

All SLs need to have a level of charisma. Usually you are the face of the organization (ambassador), and your confidence or nervousness can be perceived as the organizations well-being. A strong SL must be charismatic. It makes the SL look more competent and that will add confidence to subordinates and peers, letting them know they are in good hands. A charismatic leader also keeps the morale high in the organization. High morale will keep people working and working hard.

A SLs confidence adds to charisma. You can gain confidence from small victories. Set up those private competitions with yourself, then relish on the challenges you have overcame. When you work hard and smart toward a goal, and have accounted for all the possible mishaps, you can be confident. Whatever you do, do not confuse confidence with arrogance. If you were to ask a top executive how they expect to fair on a project and they respond proudly, "very successful," then proceed **to tell and show you why**, that exec is displaying confidence. Perhaps you are ask a fairly decent athlete how do they expect to play in their next game and what have they done to prepare. The athlete responds just as proud, then answers "very successful." Next they tell you that **no preparation or practice has been done**, and their very being at the game (**showing up**) is enough to win. That is an example of displaying arrogance. Know the difference; people are less likely to follow someone arrogant as to being confident. Arrogance shows people that there is no method to your madness and instead of having a solid, or even somewhat methodical foundation, you just stumble upon your success with sheer dumb luck. It shows that you are a ticking time bomb and continuation of arrogance will lead to a major failure or setback. Arrogance is just showing up planning to win.

A charismatic leader must also be able to inspire their followers. Potential opportunities motivate people, which boost their work ethic. In President Obama's campaign run for the 2008 election, he ran off the platform of change. Obama made sure people knew he was about changing the way things were done traditionally in the White House. Estimates of the Obama campaign fund reached almost 750 million dollars. Obama inspired enough people with the idea of change and in return he was given some change. Obama followers were fundraising, working, many even volunteering, off of his inspiration. The same concept works in all organizations, formal and informal alike. Inspiration breeds passion, as well as a purpose, and with passion people work harder. They give more of themselves than they ever thought they would, not for their leader necessarily, but for the message—the purpose, the idea, the leader speaks about. To breed this needed passion a SL must be inspiring. To become more inspiring, intricately know about the issue(s) you stand for, know how the issues affect people as a whole, and with this intricate knowledge you can speak from the heart when talking to those who wish to follow.

Charisma is an "it" factor. When there is a tie, when candidates are equally qualified, the charisma is the difference breaker. Not just in positions of leadership, but in anything. That human instinct kicks in and the biases begin. The question gets asked would "I" want to work next to this person. People want to be around other charismatic people because of that euphoric feeling. It is almost like a natural high. Go see your favorite author, musician, business leader, and community leader, whoever it is, speak or perform in person. Just the vibe you get while you are there is positive. It makes you feel as though you can do anything. That is charisma. In the workplace or on the team it works the same way, all the time. When that human instinct kicks in, which it will especially in the masses, you want to have that edgy "it" factor. You want people to want to work for you, and be around you. At every level, in every organization, one thing people love is someone who can motivate them. Create a favorable impression.

The preface encouraged people to read this guide in an environment conducive to learning. This is part of becoming a charismatic SL, conveying optimism. If you can portray that "no matter what it will be alright" attitude you are more likely to succeed in what you do. "People who are very successful have an incredible sense of optimism," says Joan Kane, a Manhattan psychologist who treats many high-powered executives. "They don't have the sense of limitations that most people have. There's no limit to their capacity to achieve and keep going. Age and family commitments don't deter them."

It is challenging to continuously be positive, particularly in today's world that is filled with so much cynicism. It becomes more difficult when everyone always has their eyes on you and everything you do is dissected. However as a SL it is something you must do. A few ways to maintain your optimism throughout the day is to always find solutions, always be grateful, and laugh at the little things in life. By continuing to comfort people in time of conflict and finding ways to solve problems you take your mind off of your own negativity and use that energy on helping others. Being grateful on the other hand entails you always remember, it could be worse. Be happy for what you have and continue to receive. This is something that helps throw your worries out the window. And finally, laugh at the little things in life. A smile will almost always brighten your mood and those around you. Keep something funny around, so in stressful times you can sit back and have a smile.

The Law of Attraction is a belief that can clearly convey optimism. This law says that whatever you think about will manifest into your life. By focusing on positive or negative thoughts, you bring about positive or negative results. According to the Law of Attraction, the phrase "I need more money" allows you to continue to "need more money." It is a negative statement, which will subconsciously have a negative impact on your mind. If you want to change this then you would focus your thoughts on the goal (having more money) rather than the problem (needing more money). This might take the form of phrases such as "I will make more money" or "I will find a job that pays very well." The latter two statements are positive and proactive. These statements have placed psychological pressures on yourself and peer pressure from your friends—if said aloud—to see if you can follow through. This now places your reputation on the line in a public setting, as well as your character, in a private one. You are now more likely to at least make an honest attempt at acquiring more money because you have challenged yourself (private competition).

Continuous optimism does one more important thing for SLs. When people rarely see you upset or promoting negative energy, they will respect it more when it happens. If you know someone who is constantly angry and complaining, then it holds no weight when they say something negative. It is who they are. You become more surprised when these people say something positive or are in a good mood. When you are always positive and in a great mood and the day comes where something has angered you and your output is negative, then everyone is paying attention. It matters because they know it must be a serious issue at hand, if the issue was able to get you outside of your comfort zone.

Never have a bad day, period! For many of the people you meet, it will be their first and only encounter with you. They do not care about your troubles, so suffer in silence. Leave them with only good things to remember about you. Think positive, speak positive, and surround yourself with positive people.

Chapter 17

LEARN TO MASTER MIND, WORDS, MONEY

By mastering these three things the amount of autonomy and control you have over yourself and in society increases tenfold. Autonomy and control may sound wicked, but it's not. Like many things, how you apply this determines the impact of the consequence.

Mastering your mind is the most important. Having confidence to stand for what you believe in when everyone around you doesn't. Having the confidence to follow your visions and ideas and taking the big risk, when all odds seemed to be stacked against you. Mastering your mind allows you to stay focused and stick to the game plan. You control the thoughts that flow through your head, the motivation, the fatigue, the pain, you can turn anything physical into mental and continue to go on as needed. Conversely, you also realize when to pull the plug on things that do not work, how to ask for help, and how to let others smarter or better at you in something take control. Mastering your mind does not mean you will never have another doubt again, but it does mean you are prepared for whatever life throws at you next. Once you have mastered your own mind the amount of confidence you exude is exponential.

After mastering your mind it is important to get your thoughts out in a manner others can understand, this is where the mastery of words comes in handy. Sometimes sounding smarter will give you the upper hand in life, even if you are wrong. Sounding smart isn't just using big words; it is having an extended vocabulary and tying together the right words that create harmonious sentences, speeches, and stories.

Words are very powerful; they are the best way for humans to exchange ideas and information, and some research has indicated that up to 90 percent of disagreements can be attributed to miscommunication. Kingdoms and wars have been won and lost with words. Having a good command of language is essential to communication and education. You must be able to manipulate words. Not to apply it in a corrupt way, but so you know how to effectively communicate what you mean to all types of people. Below is a list of ideas that are often manipulated by words. What you say is what you mean. Words matter.

Arsenal of Weapons	Gun Collection
Delicate Wetlands	Swamp
Undocumented Worker	Illegal Alien
Cruelty-Free Materials	Synthetic Fiber
Assault and Battery	Attitude Adjustment
Heavily Armed	Well-protected
Narrow-minded	Righteous
Taxes or Your Fair Share	Coerced Theft
Commonsense Gun Control	Gun Confiscation Plot

Illegal Hazardous Explosives	Fireworks or Stump Removal
Non-viable Tissue Mass	Unborn Baby
Equal Access to Opportunity	Socialism
Multicultural Community	High Crime Area
Fairness or Social Progress	Marxism
Upper Class or "The Rich "	Self-Employed
Progressive, Change	Big Government Scheme
Homeless or Disadvantaged	Bums or Welfare Leeches

Many politicians are nothing more than talented speakers. They have mastered words and can manipulate them in a way that makes you feel good after hearing them speak. Since politicians speak for groups (cities, states, countries), they have to be able to communicate an idea from thousands of people to millions. If you can speak about something halfway intellectually and make a group of people feel a desired way, you are on your way to mastering words. Since charisma can directly influence the presentation of words, it is only appropriate to continue the Obama example. President Obama's first campaign was run on the idea of hope and change. Obama's mastery of words allowed him to win the crowd over because everyone felt good when he finished speaking. Obama was not any more experienced than the opposing candidates— none of whom were incumbent's, but Obama's ability to manipulate words to his advantage allowed the president to sell the idea of what he was saying. Some circles consider this a "silver tongue." It can have a positive and negative connotation, but the expression denotes a definite ability to effectively convince with rhetoric.

Adversely, President George Bush Jr. did not have a mastery over words, or at least it seemed like he did not when he spoke publically. Throughout Bush's presidency the running joke used on Bush by comedians and radio host alike, was his inability to effectively communicate. Late night television hosts would insult Bush's stuttering or moments when he was speaking and his mind seem to draw blank, causing Bush to occasionally say things that did not make the most sense. Bush was very charismatic, so people liked him; however Bush's competency was always called into question attributed to the way he communicated.

Learn to master words and you will be able to sell anything from t-shirts to ideas. By mastering words getting a job in itself will never be anything you need to worry about. The hardest part will become getting an interview, knowingly aware after you get a chance to speak the position is yours. The more words you know the more likely you are to have a higher position in a company, this is proven. Master your language and build your vocabulary.

The third significant thing that you must master is money. By no means does being rich mean you are successful, but showing a mastery over money displays intellect and a sense of responsibility. Mastering money depict these traits to the public because of the perceived time and difficulty involved in doing so. Money is something that is hard to get but easy to lose for some. Mastering money shows you can be trusted with more serious task because of the amount of weight people place on it.

Jobs, banks, and businesses alike, use your bank account and credit score to determine risk. It may not equally correlate to your character as a person, but it's definitely used to correlate to your intellect and responsibility. If a person can be responsible with their own finances they must be smart enough to handle "this," these institutions think. Or if an account can stay above X consistently then they must be a responsible person. With an increased number of people going into bankruptcy, and a diminishing middle class, one thing is clear, people have not mastered money. The mortgage crisis and loss of jobs should not [1]matter to you. There are still people becoming rich overnight, going against the grain, and making the system work for them. Learn to master money. This does not mean you need to have a million dollars, but just getting out of debt or reducing your debt is a start. If you have no debt then you are already successful, everything you have you own. Over 50 percent of America cannot say that. By continuously creating streams of revenue and passive income you are on your way to mastering money.

> "You get better with time, so do everything
> as early as possible."

---

[1] Law of attraction, if you believe in negativity, negativity will come and vice versa.

Chapter 18

SUBMISSION→SYNERGY→WIN-WIN

Submission

True leaders know how to submit. If you left two leaders in a room and gave them a project, two things would occur. One being that both people would talk for a while and eventually figure out who is better suited for the job. The better person would indirectly take the reins and the other would fall back and support. Two, is that both people will find each other exceptionally knowledgeable and instead of picking one leader they will use interdependence and work as partners. If for whatever reason one person had to be in charge, the two will use a fair way to decide. This is what submission is about. Leaders know that a job needs to be done the right way and occasionally compromise is inevitable.

If the United States two major national parties were observed (Democratic and Republican), you would see examples of horrendous leaders. Both parties have members that are stuck on the answer being my way or the highway. That is to say, if you do not do exactly what I say and how I want it, then I will not cooperate with anything you plan to do. This makes no sense. America is one of the largest and diverse nations on earth. Compromise is the only thing everyone can possibly agree on as a country. There will rarely, if ever, be a time when all of America will agree on something. Instead however, the people elected to essentially decide the fate of the country do not act in a professional manner.

If more people in positions of power, embraced better leadership skills, solutions to problems would become copious. These are smart people; just a few of them are stuck on stupid. Being smart however does not make you a great SL. It can help, it is an attribute of a SL, but it is not the end game. It is always difficult to change and even more difficult to submit. Especially professionally, it is look on as a weakness. In politics if you change your standpoint enough you are looked at as a "flip flopper." Someone who cannot make up their mind, so surely they cannot be the leader, opponents argue. Furthermore, submitting is attacked by opponents and the media as signs of a pushover for a leader. Neither of these is true. Remember one thing SLs, you are the minority. The elite minority, so everything you do is a double edged sword. Not many fully understand your thought process or why the decisions you make are right, so there will always be some sort of negative judgment coming your way. This is the exact reason you should never be afraid to voice your opinion or change your mind on a previous stance you took. SLs are never done growing and sometimes new information is presented that causes you to rethink your feelings on a subject.

Case in point: A teacher thought a female student was his favorite. She was a very good student who always paid attention, completed all the assignments given and received good grades. The teacher admired her for this. At the students graduation the teacher shook every other students hand until his favorite student came on stage. Instead of shaking her hand he grabbed her, then gave her a hug and kiss. Everyone sat in disbelief at the teacher's action. The teacher then spoke and said "my daughter was my favorite student all year." With new information presented your feelings toward things can sway.

Synergy

Synergy is the interaction of multiple elements in a system to produce an effect different from or greater than the sum of their individual effects.

Why does it have to be a number one? You get more accomplished using interdependence and using synergy. Along that lonely path to prosperity, you will occasionally meet people headed for the same destination. SLs working with others is an activity that they find pleasure in, not discomfort. The more people you communicate with, the more information you can absorb. The following will explore how to help genuinely build synergy.

Seek first to understand, then to be understood. It is through conversation, not censorship that you change people. Labeling and placing judgment is counterintuitive because it is dismissive. In reality you just don't understand the person. Great lawyers and attorneys seek first to understand then to be understood. They usually build up their opponent's arguments and stance before they do their own. This way they have a response and course of action to every argument or defense. Investigators are alike in this aspect as well. Investigators attempt to mentally rebuild a crime scene and the order of events that took place—to better understand everything that occurred, before they even begin to form assumptions. These people—who are all often synonymous with intelligence—put themselves in their counterpart's shoes and almost try to become them. These types of people are mentally strong; they have to be, because they spend more time in the mind of another person than themselves. In turn they must have the ability to quickly process the information and their own thoughts, to 1communicate their point of view.

To some there is nothing more exciting than talking about themselves, their own experiences, and their own perspective. When trying to compromise, decompress a situation, or even come into the good graces of someone, let them talk about themselves. Not enough do people actually listen. Regardless of what it is, people will find tranquility in you if you let them get out what they have to say. They become much more receptive to your own thoughts and ideas simply because of "the rule of reciprocity." A person has taken your time and listening ear and now they feel they must do something of the same for you. They are giving you a chance to show them how alike you two are or aren't.

Facebook not only founded one of the world's most comprehensive communication platforms, they also initiated a competition that breeds a positive work climate and is ideal for

---

[1] Mastery of mind and words.

spawning innovation. This concept used by the employees at Facebook is genius. It is their own "Hackathon event." The Facebook Hackathon event is pretty simple. All engineer/IT employees or whoever else that works at Facebook can join, pull an [2]all-nighter, and [3]code. As Facebook founder Mark Zuckenberg puts it "every month or two, everyone stays up all night just experimenting with things and building things quickly. And the only rule is that you're not allowed to work on the same thing that your day job is." During this event there is no wrong answer and the only pressure is friendly competition. At the end of the day or night for that matter, certain programs made are immediately put onto the site and if some do well, the whole company benefits. Just looking at the videos of Hackathons Facebook has posted and hearing some of the employees' reactions to the event, anyone can tell how much of a morale booster this is to the company. While at the event everyone is broken off into teams and those who can't code as well, or at all, do things such as brainstorm ideas, draw out the vision, make food or drink runs and so on. Even though they may not be the actual person coding in the group, they find ways to play their position and help out. Everyone is respected throughout the process; because the main goal is to have fun and make great ideas you had at work, but couldn't work on because you were at work. The majority of employees at the Hackathons and many of the Facebook's executive management are relatively young. CEO Mark Zuckenberg is 27. Zuckenberg as well as his employees

---

[2] Staying up all night until the early morning.
[3] Building new computer programs from the ground up.

come to work in an environment laid back and constantly open to new ideas. The Facebook empire has estimates of being worth up to billions of dollars. This is synergy. Make hackathon like events for your organization to encourage innovation—doesn't have to be right, just make something.

"Submission is the caterpillar, synergy is the butterfly."

Win-Win

There are three situations that can occur whenever you work with others. There is the lose-lose. The lose-lose occurs when two opposing parties are in disagreement, no one wants to give up anything, and everyone wants everything they have asked for. In this situation the end is not more important than the means. Instead of either party getting some of want they want, they both foolishly settle for nothing. In lose-lose situations you become a loser as well as the other party. At the end of the day no one likes to lose, however it happens. Unfortunately when many people lose they mope around, blame others and begin to maliciously dislike, even hate the winner. These types of people are weak and should be avoided, and while aware of their proximity to you, ignored. They are looking at a win/lose column as a scorecard in relation to another individual. They don't care if they are actually right or wrong. They want to feed their ego by any means necessary. These are the people who have to shout to communicate their ideas, always poking out their chest, or downgrading others for that short boost of confidence. This is where the whining, complaining and pointing fingers comes from. This can be expected because these things are the last line of defense for the conventional person. It takes too much time, work and effort to find solutions or take responsibility. Remember losing, like failing is a learning experience and should be taken in stride.

A SL has a deep affinity for experiences, in specific, experiences that cause them to gain knowledge. This affinity is what drives a SL to become not only competitive, but also assertive. When a SL is proven wrong or fails at something, they become obsessed with the concept of why "right" is right and what are the steps to correct the failed attempt. A SL has their confidence in check so they don't fear taking a loss, especially when they learn from it. If the opposing person is instead focused on the concept as well, instead of their personal victory, then this proves to a SL that they both are sincerely alike. Synergy is then created because both parties can expect that the other will always argue their position or attempt something to the best of their ability with integrity, not maliciously or with feelings of personal negativity.

The following situation that can occur is the win-lose. Unfortunately this is how many people try to operate and it is counterproductive to a good work climate. Win-lose occur when one party gets the better end of a deal and the other is shorted. Sometimes people do not care enough about what the other guy is losing; they care about what they are getting. It is taking advantage of another party. The problem with this is that these wins are usually short lived. You may have gotten one over on another party however once either they see, or someone else sees your manipulative and shrewd business practices, others will be less likely to work with you. Some see this as a good business tactic, but in reality it is not. It is selfish and being selfish is a short-term proposition. In the long run you lose because (unless what you have to offer is just that one of a kind) people would rather work alongside someone they can trust and can make them feel good about a deal.

The final situation is the one that should always be the goal of attainment. The win-win. The win-win is exactly how it sounds, everyone wins. It does not mean all parties will receive exactly what they wanted out of the deal, but it does mean that they get some of what was asked for. Win-win situations work the best because both parties walk away from the deal feeling good about their decisions and become more apt to work with each other again. This word spreads like a wild brush fire. When people and organizations know that you and your team are not only good at closing deals, but also getting everyone involved most of what they want, you will become that much more valuable and sought after. This world seems to be getting smaller because of the technologies that bring everyone closer and globalization. Your reputation is what will continue to keep you in business and give you new opportunities in life. Become the person who is known to get win-wins and all will know. A win-win is synergy working at its finest.

"Teamwork makes the dream work."

Chapter 19

SEE CONFLICT AS AN OPPORTUNITY

Some people as kids were taught to turn the other cheek, ignore, or walk away from conflict. That is not how you grow as an individual or find ways to success. When conflict arises take it head on, especially when it comes to people. You learn new things about yourself and others, you learn ways to solve new problems, and you gain respect from your subordinates, peers, and superiors. Treat conflict as a way of personal growth and team growth. Conflicts are nothing more than a collision of thoughts and processes. There are only a few things that cause conflict among people. These include: miscommunication, difference of ideas—beliefs, personal insecurities—, boundaries, and expectations, whether it is yours or theirs. Conflict can also arise when someone cares too much and someone else not enough. When you take conflict head on with another person understand that sometimes you are right and sometimes you are wrong. No one knows everything, especially what another person is feeling or thinking, and from another point of view you may be wrong.

After a conflict has begun or happened and it is time to confront it do the following. Ask the person or group of people to speak to them in private. By speaking one on one to a person, often they will let down the guard that they up keep in the public eye. Briefly acknowledge there is a problem and you want to solve it expediently as possible to not only move on, but to also know what caused it so it won't occur again. After your quick spew ask the person(s) what they feel is wrong and why. Do not interrupt, face to face interaction can be sensitive to some (especially if you know you are not dealing with those trained to deal with conflict and voice their opinion in a respectful manner), and stay engage. Remember seek first to understand. After the person has gotten whatever they need off their chest, repeat back in summary what was said to you. This ensures you fully understood what they meant and how they felt so you both are on the same page. Next, integrate your thoughts into theirs to figure out where the miscommunication came from. Once the dispute is settled, both parties need to set standards of what is acceptable to ensure the same conflict does not occur again. This way of problem solving encourages positive growth between both parties. Now, you both know what triggers the other person and if conflicts occur you are both confident you can talk about the issue and figure out how to solve it in the most 3E fashion.

"May noise never excite us to halt, or confusion reduce us to defeat. Win through actions not through arguments."

Chapter 20

PERSECUTION LEADERS FACE

The elite are a group of relatively small size, which is dominant within a large society, having a privileged status perceived as being envied by others of a lower line of order.

The masses are not SLs, nor do they want to be, so they have no incentive to understand a SL, especially when it is easier to just sweep their behavior under the rug. The person who goes to the library or their study all night after work leads a life seemingly too tough and impossible for the average Joe. Maybe there is not an immediate reward seen—short-term compensation does entice the weak. Many behaviors SLs exhibit are behaviors misunderstood by the masses. Whatever the case, instead of having a mutual respect for the way someone else spends their time, people will look at a SL as someone who thinks they are better than the rest. Why don't you go out and have fun? Get a drink? Relax? They will never understand any answer a SL will provide, if they even offer one, so they will continue to just write you off, it is easier than actually thinking it through. Critics criticize, winner analyze.

Citing the 2010 National Security Strategy, the first line in the security section is a quote from President Obama's Inaugural Address (January 20, 2009).

"We will not apologize for our way of life, nor will we waver in its defense."

This United States security stance is one of humility. The U.S. will not strike first, but if attacked they will not cower. They will not feel sorry or apologize for their lifestyle either. Remember this quote when it comes to the persecution you will face. Never feel bad for the position you have worked yourself into. Continue to show some humility, but never feel bad. Today's world is ripe with opportunity, but for whatever reason many people do not take the necessary risks. There will never be a time where everyone likes you, so instead of trying to become liked, just focus on doing a great job. The following lyrics in one of infamous rapper's Jay-Z song, sums it up:

[1]"See success and its outcome, see Jesus, see Judas, see Caesar, scc Brutus, see success is like suicide, suicide it's a suicide, if you succeed prepared to be crucified...now the question is, is to have had and lost better than not having at all?"

This is true. After you reach peak levels in society and you begin to separate yourself from people, no matter how humble

---

[1] Jay Z Grammy Family, Dear Summer.

you are you will not be seen as an equal. Nothing you do will be right to some. Make peace with this early on. Don't plan on ignoring this fact because it can lead to extortion. Ignoring the fact that you are one of the best and that some people don't like you will make you blind to offers where it is certainly a lose-win situation for yourself. Instead just know how to deal with it. Just like you know you are a winner there are people who *know* they are losers and they play the role accordingly. Their only chance to feel the same satisfaction as you do when you win is to bring you down with them to their level, so you two can be losers together. Some people aren't prepared to accept success—especially someone else's. It is a crab mentality. Knowing this, you must be able to deal with unauthentic friends' who will appear, be able to sniff out cynics and cultivate a loyal inner circle.

Don't work for peoples liking, work for their respect; this way you will always have a career and a network of reliable people you can call on who at the very least can objectively see value in what you produce. The expression: you're damned if you do, you're damned if you don't, should always be contemplated before you form a course of action. Any action you make, positive or negative, will evoke different feelings for different people. *You cannot please everyone* and *everyone will not like you*. The earlier you learn this, the more content and confident you will become. By trying to continuously impress those who do not like you will start to lead you down a path of self-doubt and depression. You become the dog that is used to getting whipped, always walking with your head down and hesitant over your next move in fear of the feelings it might evoke. A SL's job is not to please everyone, it is to get the job done and lead in the most 3E way possible. When working toward something do it with integrity and bring back results. Whether a person likes you or not, will become secondary to your competence. People on the same path of success will care more about the results you generate then your personality. Results are an important denominator that bonds all organizations alike. As people progress in their work environment and seek others to work with them or for them, they will not be looking for the nicest person they have worked with—they will be looking to hire the people who were honest, result oriented and reliable. Do not get hung up on the fact that someone may not admire you personally, as long as they respect you professionally then that is all that matters. Once you become confident in your ability to do your job as one of the best, continue to work hard and let the results speak for themselves.

Persecution Illustrated:

There was once a king who was put in a terrible situation. All of the citizens in his kingdom obtained their water from a different well than the one from which he drank. The well of his subjects became tainted and as a result of them drinking from that well, all of his once-loyal followers went mad. Because everyone in the kingdom had gone crazy, they all looked at each other as if they were still normal and that the king was actually the one that had gone crazy.

Even though he tried everything in his power to help his people, his subjects would spend every day attempting to convince the king he was crazy and try different remedies to cure his madness. When the king could no longer face the treatment and couldn't bear to be so different from everyone else, he decided to give in and drink from their tainted well. When he did, he became just like them and the country, although all crazy, was happy again.

When you are outnumbered and long for affection, it is not easy to meet with such resistance. Perhaps it would be easier just to drink from their well. Well life is not supposed to be easy. You will not be measured by the easy decisions you make, but instead by the most challenging ones.

Richard Branson and Steve Jobs both made decisions in their careers that continuously made them seem crazy, get fired, or even blackballed. Their decisions should have seemed crazy because they were/are both SLs. They're also people who created and decided not to follow the status quo. In the long run both these men let the results speak for themselves.

Understand, when your confidence bumps into someone's insecurities, you will always seem arrogant. Instead of trying to fix this ill feeling someone has toward you, hang around the people who have already achieved their goals or are working on similar ones as yourself. These people will respect and admire your passion. Would you rather have a good surgeon who is nice, tries to fit in, but maybe lacks confidence, operate on you, or a self-assured surgeon who recognizes and takes pride in being one of the best? [2]"Be courteous to all, but intimate with few, and let those few be well tried before you give them your confidence."

"People fear what they don't understand and
hate what they can't conquer."

---

[2] George Washington.

Chapter 21

LEADERS

Why are there leaders? Why do we look to people as leaders? Leaders provide safety, security and knowledge. These are basic pillars to what people must have to survive in this world since its earliest times. Leaders have a vast array of problem solving skills to maneuver through any predicament. They are strong people who stand courageous and will step up to any problem or threat.

Leaders carry an enormous amount of responsibility and as a result their accomplishments grant them notoriety and profit. If you master the art of leadership you will always be taken care of. You will always have shelter, food, clothing, a great network of family and friends, and multiple places you can call home. The leaders who wish to pursue more will sacrifice more, but they are rewarded justly. It is for you to decide what your ceiling will be.

Generally speaking the world is in need for more leaders. This applies to any domain, business, or sport, you name it. Applying the tactics in this guide will not only allow others to see and accept you as the SL you are, but you will also be awarded deservingly. To highlight how significant leadership is and how the world is still in the need for more, refer back to the 2010 United States National Security Strategy:

> "Our approach begins with a commitment to build a stronger foundation for American leadership, because what takes place within our borders will determine our strength and influence beyond them. This truth is only heightened in a world of greater interconnection—a world in which our prosperity is inextricably linked to global prosperity, our security can be directly challenged by developments across an ocean, and our actions are scrutinized as never before."

This embodies a leader. As an individual what takes place within your borders is how you build yourself intrinsically. Your strength, influence, and economic security lies in your ability to produce. That truth becomes heightened once you take your talents out into the professional world around others in which you work and compete to accomplish things. Always assume the world is watching, listening and observing everything you do, therefore you will always be scrutinized. That is the public scratching the surface to ensure you are real (fool's gold) and yes your livelihood—your security will be threatened if you are not.

> Elite leadership is the ability to organize a group of people to achieve a common goal in the most 3E way.

BOOK III

MANAGEMENT

The World's Worst Boss

That would be you.

Even if you're not self-employed, your boss is you. You manage your career, your day, your responses. You manage how you sell your services and your education and the way you talk to yourself. Odds are, you're doing it poorly.

If you had a manager that talked to you the way you talked to you, you'd quit. If you had a boss that wasted as much as your time as you do, they'd fire her. If an organization developed its employees as poorly as you are developing yourself, it would soon go under.

I'm amazed at how often people choose to fail when they go out on their own or when they end up in one of those rare jobs that encourages one to set an agenda and manage themselves. Faced with the freedom to excel, they falter and hesitate and stall and ultimately punt.

We are surprised when someone self-directed arrives on the scene. Someone who figures out a way to work from home and then turns that into a two-year journey, laptop in hand, as they explore the world while doing their job. We are shocked that someone uses evenings and weekends to get a second education or start a useful new side business. And we're envious when we encounter someone who has managed to bootstrap themselves into happiness, as if that's rare or even uncalled for.

> There are few good books on being a good manager. Fewer still on managing yourself. It's hard to think of a more essential thing to learn. -Seth Godin

Plain and simple, if you are not getting what you want out of life, then you need to manage yourself better. Manage yourself first, and then watch the rest fall in place. It is never too late to start. If you are 60 years old and you have been a poor manager of yourself, then start now. You can live the rest of your life fulfilling a very important purpose, you and your happiness. Even if you have kids, start managing yourself first. You do them no good if their leader is not running at an optimal performance. Do what you must now in the short-term, turn your mind and body into one of a SL, and in the long-term everyone you come in contact with will appreciate it. A significant step toward success is *managing yourself exceptionally well*.

Thus far you have a destination and a mode to get there. Now you need to appreciate the maintenance involved to finish your journey. Properly managing yourself is nothing more than performing the appropriate maintenance on your life. Book III delves into an assortment of management skills including The Big 5. The Big 5 are all things that you have done before and continue to do. This just gives you a name and the science behind them. The Big 5 is composed of positive self-talk, visualization, planning, goal-setting, and time-management. All things you should be doing on a consistent basis.

"To improve an organization, improve yourself, then the organization will get pulled up with you."

Chapter 22

POSITIVE SELF-TALK

Christine Carter, a sociologist, says that "hugs are a really great way to boost our mood and bring us happiness." She explains "when we give and receive hugs, our body releases oxytocin, which is nature's "feel good" hormone. It brings about feelings of trust, generosity, and of course, happiness. A minimal of eight hugs a day are needed."

Did you ever think something as simple as a hug could bring about that much of a change in mood? If that works there must be other methods to release desired mental hormones. Self-talk is one. Everyone is not in a position to receive or give eight hugs a day, but everyone is in a position to use self-talk. Self-talk brings about feelings of trust, generosity, happiness, confidence, and a ton of others. No empirical evidence on this one, just anecdotal evidence from history's most successful people who all say they do it and it works. Self-talk invokes beliefs into your brain and eventually makes it a reality. To display how long self-talk has actually been around read and reflect on this quote from Lao-Tzu, a philosopher of ancient China and also seen as a deity in some cultures.

"Watch *your thoughts*; they *become words*. Watch *your words*; they *become actions*. Watch your actions; they become habit. Watch your habits; they become character. Watch your character; it becomes your destiny."

Have you ever seen someone do something in complete confidence that you perceived as irrational? Think about it. The American idol audition in which someone sincerely believed that they could sing, when the judges and the rest of the world did not. Or a friend who cooks and believes their food is the absolute best when really it tastes terrible. In the American Idol instance look at William Hung. Hung was a twenty year old college student who decided to try out for the show with no previous experience in the entertainment industry, specifically singing and dancing, the song She Bangs. The judges did not like his performance by far, but they were impressed with his positive attitude. Hung repeatedly said before and after the audition that he was going to do his best and music was something he wanted to do as a career. After being dismissed from auditions, Hung received worldwide attention and fame. Hung signed a record deal and had his foot in the door in the entertainment industry. What sold Hung is his confidence. He repeatedly told himself that he was going to do something then he did it. Another example is famed entertainer, actor, comedian, Eddie Murphy. Eddie Murphy and his brother Charlie Murphy have told the public on numerous occasions how they both knew Eddie would become successful and famous. Eddie always said growing up that he would be on TV, and that he constantly practiced his routines in front of his family. When Eddie became "big" it wasn't a surprise to his brother Charlie because Eddie always said it would happen.

Your internal beliefs affect your performance. What you believe is what it will be. There is no room for a defeatist attitude in successful cultures. This goes way past optimistic thoughts. Positive self-talk is spoken in a manner where you are about to conquer something. You have prepared for the moment and positive self-talk is just your number one fan cheering you on. You build positive self-talk by doing it daily. It can range from you telling yourself you will accomplish something in the morning, to gratifying yourself in the evening. Or just telling yourself how beautiful you are, how well you speak, even how good you smell. Self-talk helps you perform confidently, get the job done, and strike an awesome posture. Someone who is not confident can be seen from a mile away from their poor posture. Messed up hair, wrinkled clothes, looks down, and hunched over, to name a few. None of those traits remotely sound like someone who cares or who is confident. While having all of these things in check does not guarantee the person can get the job done, it sure does inspire confidence in themselves and others.

Psychologically self-talk makes you transform into what you said. If a person has low self-esteem and continuously down plays themselves, then it makes it just as easy for others to do the same. If you go to work, school, or practice, and you have already told yourself that you are no good, then there is no way to perform at a high standard. You have already given up, so exceeding your limits and pushing yourself is no longer an option. Mentally you are defeated. This works the same vice versa. If you have high self-esteem and you only talk and encourage yourself in a manner that an Olympic champion would, you become well on your way to champion results.

This same type of success from self-talk can be seen all over the cream of the crop. National leaders, entertainers, athletes, even in local leaders, teachers, firemen, police. The bottom line is that if you want something to happen—if you want to feel a certain way you have to tell yourself that. Aloud too, not just mentally. By all means if you are in a board meeting or crowded area don't start talking to yourself. This is the time to mentally reinforce yourself and say you are ready or you are the best. But at home, in the restroom, locker room, somewhere where you can get some quick one-on-one time with yourself to get mentally prepared—speak aloud. SLs should remind themselves daily it is not a mistake that they are in their present position. Tell yourself the only place to go every day is up because it is unacceptable to settle for anything less. That the spotlight is constantly on you, so your performance does not just affect you, but your followers as well. On the flip side. SLs have to be ready to tell themselves that they messed up. Be critical of yourself. Others may either be too scared to offend or not in a position to respectfully tell you your flaws. Critique yourself every night before you go to bed. What did you do right and what did you do wrong today, and how to rectify the situation tomorrow.

Here are some things you can do to work on positive self-talk. Pick five places outside of your comfort zone. Proceed to go to those places and make five new buddies (one at each stop). Every time you leave that new place, write down your thoughts before you entered and your thoughts when you exited. You don't have to become best friends with anyone, but build some sort of relationship in these foreign places, so when you leave and come back they might remember you. Do not meet people you perceive as having something in common with. If you really want to boost how confident your self-talk is, tell the people you meet what you are doing and why. Guaranteed, that the fifth time you enter your newest uncomfortable place, you will be saying more positive things to yourself than what you originally did on your first trip. You can try this exercise at the mall where there are a variety of different stores or at school where there are sure to be professors you have never met. Use your imagination and go somewhere that makes you uncomfortable.

"When will and belief combine so ardently
nothing can deny you."

Chapter 23

VISUALIZATION

Think about a time you were scared to death. Literally petrified to the point you were either shaking or in disbelief from being caught so off guard. You quickly became aroused and could not immediately respond to the situation because the unexpected event was not initially visualized.

Now revert back to an instance where you were prepared to be caught off guard. A lot of the shock value disappears from you knowing what to expect. Visualization helps you gain control of your emotional responses. This is a good way to practice arousal-control. By practicing your visualization skills you can increase your arousal-control. Think about it. Your birthday is coming up and you know your friends and family are planning you a surprise party. You know the date, the time, the place; you know what gifts you are getting and who is invited. Days leading up to the party you have already visualized a number of scenarios in your head about how everyone will pop out of corners and crevices the room has to offer to yell surprise. The big day is here and as you walk into the place where your surprise function is held, the lights come on, your friends, your family, and everyone you love is there to yell surprise, you have to almost fake being alarmed. Visualization has helped you mentally remain calm and control stimulating your body. When you visualize and practice arousal-control you can reduce anxiety.

A great example of reducing anxiety can be seen in fighters. Fighting is something that can rev almost anyone up, but not fighters themselves. Fighters visualize themselves train, and visualize things their opponent can do while they train. When the fight occurs many fighters become relaxed and they feel as much at home in their comfort zone as you would watching it on TV. In fact some people can become more aroused from watching the fight, than the fighter themselves in the fight. Work on your visualization skills and you can improve your arousal-control in all aspects of your life.

Visualization also builds strategy, muscle memory, and improves your confidence. Hopefully you think before you do most activities. If you do, then you know there are often alternate ways of doing things. By visualizing you are just figuring out the best strategy to proceed. Visualize enough about the same thing and you build your muscle memory around that. How do you get home? You might not think about that every day because you know your way home. However when you first moved to wherever you live you constantly visualized how to get back home once you left. You didn't want to get lost. You visualized, formed a strategy, along with muscle memory, until it was not even a thought, you just knew where you were going (unconscious competence). Once you develop that muscle memory and have one less thing to consciously think about you start to understand how visualization can help build confidence. After you have rehearsed something over and over again in your head, it will feel like it is seamless when you actually do it. Not saying that it will be. Sometime people can overestimate or underestimate things, but every time you go back and visualize the activity it gives you more confidence at your next attempt. Build visualization on your positive self-talk exercise. The first time you go outside your comfort zone, you can only visualize so much. After your first experience, that you will live through, you realize things aren't that bad and you may have overestimated how nervous you could be. You visualize a better strategy for next time, you visualize what people will say to you, what you will say to them, conversation starters, and so on. Now on your second trip you have a strategy and a boost of confidence.

One way to illustrate how powerful the human mind is and how profound visualization can be is by reading Dr. Harold R. McAlindon's, Success Unlimited, 1978. Inside there is a short story, Reflections on Human Potential, which demonstrates why you can do things if you believe you can. A railway employee in Russia accidentally locked himself in a refrigerator car and was unable to escape. Once he realized he was stuck, he started to think he would freeze to death. He scribbled sentences on the wall of the car as his body became numb, he became colder, and he wrote that he was "slowly freezing to death...I can hardly write..these may be my last words." He was found dead but the temperature of the car was 56 degrees because the freezing apparatus was out of order. There was no physical reason of his death. He was the victim of the illusion that his own mind had created. His mind convinced his body that he was freezing to death and won.

Visualization works in the opposite way as well. It can help cope with pain and improve rehabilitation. When you are cold, visualize being warm, and when you are tired visualize being excited. It may not be the cure all, but it can help get that extra edge for that extra hour you need to study or work. Lessons learned from Dr. McAlindon's story were to realize the power of the mind and never underestimate it. Your mind creates your future and your possibilities. Most people underestimate their ability and potential. People do not appreciate how much more they are capable of contributing. You are better than you perceive, and your duty is to assert this impact.

"All things are created twice, mental and physical."

Chapter 24

PLANNING

In life, especially in the business world, you are on a crusade. The campaign is the job market. The campaign is striving toward your visions, goals, and aspirations. The campaign is doing what you want when you want, not thinking outside the box, but eliminating the box. If you are not proactive, you become just like everyone else. Most of the global population is losing this campaign. From impoverished nations with hunger problems, to one of the greatest nations ever on this planet— constantly edge near a downward spiral because of the economic and job situation. Everyone gets it, things are tough, this is not the "good ol' days" where goods were cheaper, jobs brought people in, molded them into the worker they needed, then kept not only that worker employed, but that families children employed for future generations. With the expansion of capitalism and globalization things have changed. There are certainly still an abundance of companies that keep these old school values and take care of their own, but it is no longer the norm, nor is it the mainstream expectation. You now know the worldwide situation, so what is next? Are you going to sit stagnant and wait for another person to reach down and [1]pull you to the top? You won't sit stagnant; it isn't gratifying enough for people like you, as opposed to getting on the grind and pushing yourself physically and mentally past your limits. Past your limits is what it takes to be successful these days. Putting money in the stock market and becoming rich in a week is a weak way of thinking and a thing of the past. Getting rich quick should not be your plan, but planning to get rich is a very viable option even today. Become a SL and plan for your success. Planning will never take away your experience from paying dues. What it will do however is make you work smarter, not harder. You can never expect to become or maintain being the best of anything if you have not planned for it. There are too many variables and obstacles in life already and as you climb your respected ladder to the top more pressure gets added to you.

---

[1] Even if that was the case and the only thing people had to do was reach their hand back up, more than half of the population would not want to. Apathy and laziness plague the masses today.

Plan Your Million Dollar Vision

The [2]average American full-time job consist of a 40-hour workweek, the average student might spend around 30 hours a week on class time. During this time what you do can determine your value to the organization. Those who work all those hours hard and smart will be the people to more than likely keep their job and move up in the organization.

Now apply this same logic to planning, finding a career, starting a business, or becoming a millionaire. When you begin to plan something you must remember "Rome wasn't built in a day." Or in a few weeks for that matter, but when Rome was created it became the most adored and vast empire of its day and is still admired even today because of its longevity and illustrious lifespan it had. To become successful, even to become a leader, you must plan. Write, write, write, what are you strengths, areas of opportunity, and who are you. Read, read, and read, it is understandable not to know something because you are agnostic of it. It is not understandable to stay complacent when you know there are things in this world that you do not know, but are beneficial in the campaign to creating yourself as a SL and becoming prosperous. Confused eh?

---

[2] 40-hour workweeks in America are now hardly considered average. Those 40 hours barely cover sustainment. In the competitive job market these days, many people work 50-60 hours a week and some of those hours are not compensated. That is what it takes to move up in the world today and be considered a SL. Students in law school put more time in class and studying than 40 hours a week. If that is their standard and threshold of working as a student, some full-time employees at 40 hours a week don't stand a chance against this type of individual upon their graduation.

Despite the context in which it was used, Donald Rumsfield stated it best, "there are known knowns, and known unknowns, then there are the unknown, unknowns." Can you agree that you do not know everything there is to know in this world? Can you also agree that there is a possibility that in those things you do not know, some of the information might not only be beneficial, but may also be the key to you elevating yourself to a new level mentally? These things you do not know about, are in books, are online, and are in those who have had the chance to experience life in different ways and now seek to mentor. How much time are you using to plan out your life? When looking for a career, planning is spending that same amount of time you would otherwise be working—to plan. That is a 40-hour week.

Constantly these phrases are shouted, "there aren't any jobs out there, or nobody is hiring." The folks who say this have let their own cynicism take over and have forfeited their autonomy. Ask the person who says these things, where have you looked? The common answer is "EVERYWHERE." That is hard to believe. Everywhere includes India, China, and Dubai. It includes Switzerland, Russia, and Japan; just to name places— some of which—that have robust economies that are hiring the right people. It is understandable that the economy is down and that the job market is tough in the United States. There are people out there with Ph.D.'s who can't find a job. However take a more holistic approach when looking at this. Plan. That's right as simple as it sounds; it is actually rarely practiced and slightly hard to do. If you want a good career or a job at all, put in 20-40hours a week on that task. Have some hours spent toward revising resumes', [3]researching company profiles, applying to numerous jobs (that add experience to your career), setting up appointments for interviews, mentor searching, networking, following up (thank you calls/emails for interviews), engaging in complementary or volunteer services for organizations to build your resume and showcase your talents, and reading up on what employers are looking for. While all of these tasks may seem trivial, it is what it takes to get a job these days in this tough economy. However if this is done correctly, it is assured not only will you be able to get a job, but you will be courted by a number of employers giving you the ability to choose who you will work for.

If you have never gotten the job you want post interview it is very likely your fault. There are very few, if any, companies, teams, communities, etc. who would not want a SL on their roster. Your goal whether you are job searching, looking for funding, or selling a good, is to get a listening ear. To get past all the emails, automated calls, and paperwork, to an actual person of power, or a person who can relay the message. Successful people value action, and if they stop what they are doing long enough to listen the words they hear need to have value. When people are looking for someone to fill a position of any type, a long expensive interview process begins, and each

---

[3] Doing the due diligence on a company profile, takes hours upon hours itself. If every time you walk into an interview, you know the extensive intrinsic and extrinsic information about a company profile and the leadership there, your chances to become hired are increased tenfold. One of many things this shows employers is that you are a self-starter. As stated before many organizations do not have the time or money to train employees in everything, so if you are perceived to get things done on your own, you become much more valuable.

applicant adds more time and money to this. When organizations are not looking for any extra help or business, it becomes even tougher and the window of opportunity to speak becomes even smaller. Sometimes in both situations the people you need to speak to become highly inaccessible. To combat this, you do your homework. Before you approach an organization you need to know everything about them. Their purpose, mission, short-term goals, long-term goals, problems they have encountered and overcome, future problems they might incur and solutions, how your history or skills can be of immediate value to them and how you plan to grow and develop in the organization. These are just the basics, a SL will also know about the people who have had their hopeful position in the past, the background of the interviewer/person they are speaking with, things that person have done successful with the organization, and a laundry list of intellectual questions to ask about the organization's current stance or plan of dealing with a current/future situation. If you have not gone into speaking engagements and business engagements with this type of attitude and knowledge then you are wrong. If you have received a job, a chance of some sort without displaying this type of knowledge then you are already expendable whether you know it or not.

Organizations are similar to a well sought after woman. This woman is intelligent, secure, loyal, and one of the most beautiful people you have ever seen. Her potential is limitless and in many ways even you know she may be too good for you. Right now in this time, she does not need you as much as you need her. However this woman is not against a relationship with the right person. Despite this she does not casually date. She will only date those who are husband material. Now why would any well sought after woman (or man) in our society (respectively for you) want you? What do you have to offer to continue to make them better in life? From the time you meet this person, they are looking at what a relationship right now and what will a relationship in ten years will be like. Can they grow and get old with you? Well if you are trying to woo this sought after person and you know nothing about them and you did not even make an effort to find out, why should they take their chances dating you? It's unreasonable. Even if you do get a chance to meet this person and they show slight interest, give you a lunch date (interview) perhaps even two, and you never once bring any questions about their future or your own to the table, then YOU have made it clear it was not meant to be. In the premature stages of a relationship if you can show this type of care and intimacy to an organization, there is no reason not to bring you on board. The can do attitude of a SL is already so hard to find. That same attitude will put you ahead of people currently in an organization. Furthermore, if an organization already has a roster full of the right people at that moment, they will still want to add you because you can continue to keep their winning tradition.

This leads right into planning for your own business. When you can get to the point where employers are contacting you for your work, you must know exactly what it is you offer and how valuable it actually is. If it is something of value find a market where you can sell your skills. This can be done part-time as a consultant or full-time if the demand is high enough. The television show Shark Tank is an excellent display of people who often just fall into becoming a business owner. Many of the people who come on this show either still have or had a full-time job while starting their business. These people decided to go above and beyond. After they worked their job hours, they went home and worked on their own businesses, even went to school or read on how to keep growing and improving their business and themselves. Most of these business owners even say one of the contributing reasons they started their own business is because people started to contact them in high volume wanting whatever it is they had to offer. Financially it just did not make sense to continue to work their full-time job for someone else, when their own business had the capability to make more money if more time was invested. These people plan, read, etc., then come to the show to find a platform and mentor amongst other things. For those out there interested in starting or growing your own business, what have you done today?

If someone were to ask you to spend 40 hours a week for three months to come up with a way to make a million dollars, could you? After reading this guide and instilling the practices into your daily life the answer should be yes. People don't have a chance to make a ton of money because they do not have the free time associated to brainstorm and create a game plan for such ideas. Furthermore they do not have the time and resources to always pursue that plan. So instead you get those who have random genius thoughts and while everyone agrees it is a good idea, it falls to the wayside because there is no perceived time to act upon it. Leisure time is a pleasure of the wealthy, and this is a reason why the rich get richer and the poor get poorer. If people had and dedicated a ton of time to planning financial routes of prosperity, then the chances of it happening would increase. While not initially wealthy, some of the business folks that have created and changed markets are/were young. The stories of Facebook, Microsoft, and Apple founders are already infamous. [4]One thing all these people had in common was leisure time. Generally the issue with youth who have the free time is that they are not mature or focused enough to dedicate all of their time to an idea, a realistic and viable business or technology. Although when the youth do spend their time on these endeavors many strike gold. The average age of business startups in America is 26. Develop a planning process to ensure the time it takes to become prosperous is fully accounted for.

People don't become millionaires because they don't spend the time it takes investing in that. Planning must be looked at the same way. If you really want a million dollars, put a million dollar effort forth. While it is definitely not easy or a shortcut, there is a path, and if it were easy everyone would be doing it. In the 90s it was ridiculously "easy" to make money in the stock market, thus you saw everybody doing it.

Chase 50k. If you become the person good at getting $50,000, those who can't make it will pay to see how it's done. If you can market the idea correctly, according to the statistics of people in poverty, surely you can turn that $50,000

---

[4] There is a great deal of things to contribute to the success of these individuals, this is just one.

into a million dollar idea. How much time reflecting are you willing to put into it?

Have Vision, Plan Your Work, and Work Your Plan

Every day a personal planner or calendar of some sort should be looked over. After spending time reflecting, write out a game plan for the upcoming week with the necessary improvements in your planner. Your planner should be an extension of you. It is your second bible. The sick feeling you get after losing your keys, wallet, or perhaps leaving the house with the iron on, should be the same feeling you have if you are away from your planner for too long. You must discipline yourself to treat the words you write into it as legal contracts. You do not have to show anyone your planner; it is your map to prosperity. If this is done on a weekly basis, you will see yourself begin to become more 3E, it will be second nature.

Your planner should contain a variety of things. For starters, there must be a constant reminder of your passion. Your heart and soul has to be into whatever it is your doing. Write your mission statement and purpose at the front and back of your planner, respectively. In addition to this, write your go to quote or experience that will make you work and then work harder. Creating the passion is by far the toughest thing to do in this process because of the distractions and diversions this world has to offer. Only you know what can rile you up, find that thing and make it your go to move in times of distress.

Always remember one thing with your planner, plan all the way to the end. Plan all the way to the end of your day, week, and year. Contrary to some beliefs, this does not take out [5]spontaneity in your life. On the very first page place your goals down for the year. In the notes section write down your five-year goals, ten-year goals, and twenty-year goals. Remember you are the only person who will see this. Your yearly goals and five-year goals are considered short-term. These are the building blocks to the top, the top being your long-term ten to twenty year goals. Sure these are likely to change, however sitting back and reflecting on your life goals and writing it down, are the preliminary steps to your prosperity.

Set aside some time daily to brainstorm about different ideas you have. Some individuals can come up with their mission statement and a set of goals in as little as a week while others may take months. It doesn't really matter how long it takes you as long as it is true to what you feel as a person and it coincides with what you want out of life. After these are made, and recorded into your planner, next enter the top goal(s) you have for the year. One thing to remember when making your goal(s) is that you will continue to learn new information throughout life and life experiences will occasionally alter the way you perceive things. If new opportunities arise that you didn't plan for, take a hard look at them. If these new opportunities align with your values, allow you to progress toward your main goals, and serve purpose then alter your stance.

---

[5] By planning to the end you know when you have blocks of free time, or activities you may be on the fence about participating in. Both of these times are excellent occasions to get away or go do something completely random.

For example, your ten-year goal may be to become the mayor of your city. To do this you lay out a post grad plan that consist of going to law school, practicing law in the city long enough and good enough to become a district attorney, then after a few big cases run a mayoral race. Well what if after college you get a chance to work on Capitol Hill in the political realm or post law school you have an opportunity to work for the current mayor. Both opportunities alter your path and the set short-term goals of practicing law, but they are both great courses that can eventually lead you to the same long-term goal.

The best way to predict the future is to invent it. Don't allow variables or obstacles to determine what your outcome will be. Set your sights on what you want, and create a realistic game plan. At times you may need to adapt, but for the most part stick to what you have written up. Stick to the research you have done, because in times of extreme pressure the only things you have to fall back on is your game plan and training. If you have been keeping yourself honest and honing the foundation to your prosperity, then you will have nothing to worry about. Pressure is only felt by those who don't know what they are doing. You plan to be a SL and you plan prosperity.

Life is a chess game. No matter what field you are in, who you are surrounded by, or your role, you must remember life is a chess game. Chess is a slow played strategic game. Those who play chess well know all about sacrifice, patience, adversity, vision, adaptability, and smart work. The best chess players can beat you in the first few minutes even if the game does not end for another half an hour. This is because they will have already analyzed your style of play and have formatted a plan in their head to beat you. The plan resembles the bull and the matador. The matador knows the bull hates the color red and will charge at it. In chess some players allow what seems like easy access to their king, and opposing players usually charge at the opportunity to check them. But what lies behind the red veil, nothing, a trap. Chess players spend the whole game trying to figure out ways to gain leverage over an opponent. This can be taken in a positive light. In life, you need to realize not only what you want and how to get there, but what can stop you, what are the distractions—the traps. Calculate and plan areas where you might expect losses and what course of action to take when it happens. Write it all down to the very end. Life is a marathon not a sprint, so plot your points to finish accordingly.

"Those who fail to plan, plan to fail."

Education

This is one of those topics that has countless theories and is debated in every country, state, or even tribe. There is not enough time to teach everyone everything, so curriculums are formatted to teach the basics of what that area of responsibility feels you should learn. The world needs to give itself some credit though. With globalization and new technologies such as the internet, more information is spread and easier to access than ever. Countries can now outsource jobs to other countries that may expertise in an area because of the different education system they have. Education in itself is not bad; it is something to always pursue. However there are some things about formal education you must come to the realization of.

Formal education does not make everything in life ok. In America, formal education began to flourish after child labor laws went into place. After the laws were enacted a plan had to be established as to what to do with all the children out of work. The answer, school. School, a place to teach and reward children who accepted: truth comes from authority; intelligence is the ability to remember and repeat, accurate memory and repetition are rewarded, non-compliance is punished, and to conform intellectually and socially. Even the bell in between classes has been argued to symbolize the bell you would hear at factories to start or stop certain parts of work. According to Seth Godin,

> "Part of the rationale to sell this major transformation to industrialists was that educated kids would actually become more compliant and productive workers. Our current system of teaching kids to sit in straight rows and obey instructions isn't a coincidence--it was an investment in our economic future. The plan: trade short-term child labor wages for longer-term productivity by giving kids a head start in doing what they're told. Large-scale education was never about teaching kids or creating scholars. It was invented to churn out adults who worked well within the system."

Formal education does not help you find a career, it grows yourself. The best thing a formal education is capable of doing is to give you options in life. For example, when you have a college degree you give yourself the option of striking out on your own and doing something totally unrelated to what you have studied. If that option fails you can always go back to the field in which your degree is in and find some kind of work. With a master's or Ph.D. you always have the option to go teach. These points about education are not meant to undermine it in any way. They are made to help you understand that education is not the end-all to life and it will not save you from any situation, it can however provide alternatives. There are plenty of people who pursue education in the hopes of becoming financially free and autonomous upon that freedom, just to find out that by the time they graduate, said person becomes a slave to their debt and works the better part of their youth to pay back the money spent on the education. The issue with formal education and the parameters it restricts you to upon graduation is that you use up all of that leisure time you have as a youth. Usually this is the same time people have the time and freedom to pursue things in life. Like everything else, have a plan when pursuing formal education.

"Knowledge is NOT power. *The application of knowledge is power.*"

Chapter 25

GOAL-SETTING

Now you have a purpose, a mission, and a set of goals you want to accomplish. This all sounds wonderful, but how are you going to get there. By working hard, smart, being effective, and efficient. Yes, these are all things you need to do in the process, but you also have to break your goals down to the most minute details. This is why planning is so important. Why having a purpose in general is important—because you use your time working in the most efficient manner to accomplish your goals.

The Process

You hear about the path to success and to reach the top you need to follow the signs. What signs? Where? Your goals are the signs on the path. When it comes to achieving your purpose, accomplishing your goals, and receiving everything that you have ever worked for, you must always remember one thing, the process. The journey, paying dues, whatever anyone calls it; it is a process, *the process*. Often times, especially while people are younger, they will not respect the process. People do not like to respect the process for one reason, it sucks. It cannot be said any other way. Most processes do suck because whatever it is you are trying to reach at the end of that tunnel is being safeguarded by a group of people who do not want to let just anyone in. Those who have never had any sort of success will not, cannot possibly understand this. Everything is a process however and by owning and attacking the process, you can not only make it competitive, but also fun. Once you have reached what others consider your pinnacle, no matter how you previously felt, good or bad, you will turn into the guardian of your craft. You too will influence the difficulty of the process on the next person and whether intentional or not, you will make it harder for the next person. First because you are a SL. As a SL you can only go above and beyond, so whatever the previous marks were for greatness, you will far exceed it, thus upgrading what is consider the entry level. This will affect the group of people in the process behind you. Secondly, once you realize that the respect of your craft, or any craft for that matter, is built upon the people you have working in the community—you will take ownership and ensure the next people that come along, parallel the community's values and are deserving of it or even your livelihood can become at stake.

How Process

You cannot set goals for things you have no control over and qualify as sheer luck. Everyone wants to win the lottery, but that does not mean it should appear on your goal sheet. Set goals for things you have direct control of. Things such as: how many days you will work out this week, how much money you will save this year, or what kind of relationship you will build with your co-workers. These are all things you have control over. Your goals can revolve around anything, but try to make them the essential things in your life. This way you maintain a level of sincerity and continuously attack the process of completion. By understanding and utilizing the process of goal-setting, you add another tool to your professional kit. SLs must know how to task their team and understand goal progression. You can only learn this through practice and patience. Understanding goal progression is a combination of a clear comprehension of where you want to go, what you need to do to get there, and how long it will take. It is being patient and paying your dues. Very rarely do you see overnight success, so valuing this process supports you when things seem to happen gradually instead of all at once—like most people want.

Segmenting

If your goal is too big, it will become frustrating trying to accomplish it—if you ever do accomplish it. Segmenting will alter the way you perceive large goals and the process associated with those goals. Segmenting ensures your goals are: specific, measureable, attainable, relevant and timely [1](S.M.A.R.T.). So that $100,000 lottery ticket may just be a

---

[1] Paul J. Meyer describes the characteristics of S.M.A.R.T. goals in *Attitude is Everything.*

thing of luck and chance, setting a goal to save $100,000 is not. Segmenting, combined with the right job and right timeframe, makes specifically saving $100,000 a very attainable and realistic goal.

- **Specific**
  - o What do you want to achieve? How will you achieve it? Why is it important to you? Clearly define the outcomes you want.
- **Measurable**
  - o Establish concrete criteria for measuring your success. Use actual numbers, target dates, or specific events to indicate when your goal has been achieved.
- **Attainable**
  - o Your goals should push you past your comfort point, but you should still be able to attain them with effort and commitment.
- **Relevant**
  - o Your goals should be important to you. Likewise, you should have the ability to directly impact them. Don't set goals that aren't significant or that you can't do anything to impact achievement.
- **Timely**
  - o Your goals should have a time element established. This will keep you on track and prevent you from simply pushing a goal off

infinitely into the distant future. It should matter now and you should have a sense of urgency about it.

Milestone Achievement Process

A small goal gives you something concrete to focus on. After completing a small goal you will have the satisfaction of a job well done, you learn to be successful—and to get used to it, you have something to check off your to do list, and you will inspire yourself to go forward. Look at a common goal and milestone it. Losing weight. You want to lose 50 pounds, this is the big goal. Losing weight involves eating right and exercise. To segment you say you will work out four times a week and eat only baked or grilled foods for the next six months. Further segmenting, you need to create milestones. One milestone can be to lose two pounds a week. Segment further; run at least one mile a day. Further, run the same mile faster every week. More segmenting, finish your last lap faster, keep going, finish the last 100 yards faster, continue, finish the last two steps faster. This is how you segment goals and create milestones for yourself. The self-gratification you will receive will be astounding. You will begin to get use to this success and it will become second nature.

Peak Meter Resetting (PMR)

After you reach that point where you feel you are giving it your all, whether it is physical or mental, get it done! You do not have to go far past the point just pass it. These are the goals you set in a moment's notice. One more second less, one more step further, five more minutes working instead of sleeping, something. After your peak meter resets your confidence will rise. That wow feeling will kick in and you will feel good just knowing that you have done something new and something you did not think you were capable of. Do this with everything in life. Before you know it your new standards will be well above your old ones. The body and mind has to be trained to pass its comfort zone and the more you do it the [2]easier it will be. This is why ironmans, triathlons, tough mudders, even 5k runs are so popular. All these events take people who may have otherwise thought they could not do it or were unsure and makes them go to completion. Then these same people train harder for the next one or a different event, preparing for a better time or longer distance. These people are PMR. These are often the same people who take that discipline into their professional lives and see multitudes of success. PMR is not solely used physically. When facing adversity in life and building mental toughness, past events can and will increase your threshold mentally to what you are capable of dealing with.

PMR works because of your perception. Perception is not only reality to others when they observe you, but it is also a

---

[2] Or at least it will be a more comfortable feeling.

reality to you and how you view the world. Your views will not change a situation, but they can change how you feel about a situation, thus enabling you to cope. Once they change how you feel about a situation, the Law of Attraction goes to work. To manage your perception, take the "Forrest Gump" approach. In the movie Forrest Gump, Forrest was optimistic many times when others were not because of the way he managed his perceptions. For example, while Forrest Gump was serving in the Vietnam War his unit was constantly on the go marching, always in danger, continuously in unknown territory, and wet for four months straight under heavy rains. Even if this was not a Vietnam warzone, it still sounds like unfavorable conditions for most. Forrest Gump perceived his experience a different way. Forrest perceived his time in Vietnam by describing it as there always being someplace to go, always something to do, and a chance to not only see the countryside, but also go through every kind of rain there was. Take the "Forrest Gump" approach in the way you perceive things.

Goal-setting Works

Goal-setting does work. Believe in it, trust in it, live by it. Here is the six ways goal-setting works.

1. **Focuses attention**
   - It's possible to be busy without being very effective. Segmenting gives you no other

choice, but to do things step-by-step to reach your goal.

2. Prioritizes effort

- When you have your daily, weekly, monthly, yearly, short-terms goals written, you will clearly be able to see how it prioritizes your effort to reach those long-term twenty year goals.

3. Enhances persistence

- Every day you should have a list of goals written down. Even if it is just one or two goals on a Saturday and Sunday. On Sunday, your goal can be to read one page of the newspaper. At least the goal is written and you do it, it will breed persistence.

4. Promotes new learning strategies

- Things are always changing and it does not matter how much you respect the process, SLs always want to do things in a more 3E manner. By having your goals written down it encourages you to always think about them and their completion. Spending that reflection time on your goals will eventually help that light bulb above your head click, to show a better way of attaining that sought after goal.

5. Reset focus on the future

- Whether you complete all or some of the goals you set out for in a given month or year, it still will not change what your long-term goals are. You continue to develop alternate game plans to get you where you want to be.

6. **Turns weaknesses into hobby**

- Instead of giving up on things you are not good at, that you may want to be better in, make it a goal to put time away for it in an informal setting. When it is informal you can find ways to have fun with it, thus turning it into a hobby.

Fast Food Mentality

Many people have a fast food mentality. If you have ever worked in fast food or just paid attention to the people that do, you can easily spot what a fast food mentality is. The fast food industry has a high turnover rate amongst entry-level workers. This is not the chain restaurants fault, it is the workers fault. There aren't many people who go into the fast food industry at an entry level and plan to make a career out of it. To many it is just a job, and for some it is a job that they have been in for years with no advancement. No planning and no goal-setting, thus no advancement. After enough time of complacency, these people could not even imagine being promoted. Getting a raise yes, but being promoted, no. Even when some of these people get promoted to a supervisory position, they are in disbelief or feel they have now reached their pinnacle. This is the fast food mentality. All fast food employees do not have this mentality by any means, but the high turnover rate does more than suggest that many do. This mentality is unhealthy. Eventually it displaces a person's thought value on themselves to society. This mentality can be seen in every industry and craft at entry level and middle level positions.

Think about working in the fast food industry with goal-setting in mind. An outline of short and long-term goals and a respect for the process. This is a loose example to get the picture, not to take everything verbatim. Let's say you start working at fast food chain ABC at the age of 14. You are making minimum wage and it sucks. You work here all summer, weekends, and even some weeknights during the school year. While all your friends are out or involved in different activities, your activity is work. However you knew when you applied to ABC the work would probably not be the most fun, especially for a teenager. The contemplation of having your own spending cash is not the only thing that appealed to you as a kid, but the belief of ownership has plagued your thoughts for years. ABC has been your favorite restaurant to eat at since you can remember. Your family eats there together once a week, as well as your friends and their families. You feel almost at home with ABC, so employment there was not really a problem especially to a person like you who has never been scared of a little hard work. Not just that, but you want to own an ABC one day. You love everything about the place. You initially get the job at ABC because management has seen you there with your family and friends for many years. They know you are a good kid in the community and they don't mind the extra help. You tell your parents, the owner, or maybe your high school leadership teacher about your thoughts to own ABC, and they begin to mentor you on the process. Before you even start working you have a list of short and long-term goals you need to accomplish to own ABC. So you begin the process at the tender age of 14, working what seems to be a terrible job. You think your pain is something special, but truth be told many people are going through the same thing in their twenties and thirties and so on in new organizations trying to build their reputation from the ground up. At least now at 14 this feeling of the process can integrate into your values and set your PMR at a level unrivaled by competitors when you get older and advance.

In the short-term, ages, 14-18, your goals are as followed: learn every position the store has to offer at an entry level, integrate fully into ABC, and attack the process. Learning every entry position is knowing how to cook the food, clean the store, cashiering, and bagging the food. This includes grasping the policies, rules, and regulations of each position as well. In your teenage years you probably can only work a set amount of hours in most places, so that means a lot of learning you do will be complementary, but once again getting used to this just raises your PMR.

Complementary service is good. It does two things; first it integrates you into ABC. When all of your close friends and life become a part of ABC you take ownership of it. Once you take ownership of it and start to become a SL, your team will do the same. Instead of having a revolving door of workers, the people who are employed at ABC with you will want to continue operating there because of the camaraderie you all build. Even money will not become a deterrent at this point because everyone sees the big picture and everyone is grinding together. Concurrently, the superiors in the organization will start to take notice that you truly care about ABC. Next, by providing complementary service, you can mark it off on your resume as an internship. Think about when you did your first internship. Were you 14? With the economy today, people are in their fifties doing volunteer work, complementary services, and interning. There is nothing wrong with that either because that is what it takes to succeed and to have continued success, but credit has to be due to the 14-year-old who does it then. Now by "interning" at ABC, donating your time complementary so young, it increases your PMR.

Your last short-term goal is to attack the process. Instead of thinking how terrible work is every day, you go to work looking forward to seeing everyone because not only do have a work relationship with your teammates, but they have also turned into your friends. In essence, you have built that intimate relationship. The daily and weekly goals you set for yourself, and your supervisor sets for the team are seen as fun competition. During the week it is slow, so you have the time to learn new positions or methods to become 3E at work. You learn how to clean the store faster, thus allowing you to go home earlier when you are off. You learn how to count money better, and how much of what type of food for certain times of the day needs to be cooked, based on popularity. All things that most people only learn in a formal school setting with a specific background. You enjoy interacting with new customers and seeing the daily customers who make up the community. All this is practice because when the weekend comes and ABC is busy from sun up to sun down, the real competition begins. You and your team make it a game to get people in and out happily, then cleaning the restaurant, so you all can go home and enjoy your night at a decent time. This is the short-term attack.

From ages 18-22, you begin to transition from your short-term goals to your long-term goals, and the idea of college looms. Whether you go to school or not does not really matter here, you know your long-term goal(s) and if school is needed then by all means go. By this time you should know all the entry-level positions at the store and you should be able to run the store smoothly if the supervisor is not there. At age 18, four years in working for the company, this becomes either your primary or secondary school—depending on college plans. Now it is time to learn the store manager(s), operators, and owner's positions, respectively. The goals, these four years, will rival anything you can learn in a school house, by experience. Here you will learn all about accounting, economics, marketing, sales, communication, etc. These goals include: learning how to stock for the week, month, year, how to reach sales targets, communicating to the public the news around your store and company, who to hire/fire, leading a team, competition, and so on. After the next four years here at ABC, you should know everything. Even on a structural level.

Ages 22-24, goals for the company should equate going out to get your masters. By now you should definitely be working for the company, not just the store. With the knowledge you have at 22 you can and should be traveling for the company, helping to open other stores in different areas. You are now a true ambassador, embodying everything the company stands for and even helping to shape their stance. In between opening stores you must continue to provide that complementary service. Instead now you ask to join meetings on a larger level (store owners who meet), you take initiative to start campaigns to help with sales, change menu options, or even make technologies and interfaces at ABCs everywhere easier to use. You do your research in the food industry and find out the next big thing that people would love restaurants to offer. It has not even been ten years since numerous fast food chains have started to use milkshake machines to make and sell one of the most popular items on countless menus everywhere. Yes, you do all of this in two years. Just like a student trying to earn their master's will spend literally all of their time studying and researching, you will as well. Except a major difference is that your PMR is already extremely high from doing these same things when you were 14. Attacking this is not even seen as a chore, you are having fun. You love ABC and the people who work for it, you now love the idea of hard work and through trial and error you have begun to work smart. Every day you are just checking off more boxes to become closer to your vision of owning an ABC. Your thesis or final project will be what you can create or how much money you can save for ABC.

To fast forward this example, by 24 you have already worked in the same company for ten years. If you have put money away for retirement and saved, you should be doing pretty well off in relation to the average 24-year-old. After a few more years of learning, [3]shaking hands, and a few more rounds of golf, you will soon be one of the youngest owners ABC has ever had. Why? Because you had a plan. After almost twenty years on a job, no matter how old you are when you start, if you have a plan, a set of short-term and long-term goals, and you attack the process, you will succeed. At 34, from working at fast food chain ABC, you might be in a position to retire. This is not unbelievable. At 17, teenagers enter the military, work twenty years and some retire at the age of 37. 37 is not old. That is the start of another career if you want and once you do, this time you will have a pocket full of money to pursue what you want without fear of financial constraints and a PMR that is unrivaled. Once you reach this, almost everything you do in life will seem easy.

"20 years from now you will be more disappointed from
the things you didn't do than by the ones you did
do…Explore, dream, discover." -Mark Twain-

---

[3] At high levels in business people want to know they can work with you. The intimate relationship must be present or you will be out of business. That community is what will bring synergy.

Chapter 26

TIME-MANAGEMENT

"**S**tudies have shown that good time-management and organization skills are among the habits most highly correlated with success. In a 2002 article from College Student Journal, Garavalia and Gredler point out that at the college level utilization of time-management and organizational tools is more closely linked to grade-point average and post-graduation success than are SAT scores. Deducing these results back to younger students, you can see that the earlier students begin to manage their time, the better off they will be in the long run."

It does not help you to have all the skills and to be on the trajectory of a SL if you cannot manage your time. This is a very difficult thing to do and how you manage your time will tell a lot about you to the outside world. Be careful with whom you associate and where you speak. How you spend your time sends a message, so be selective. Maintain the dignity of your position. Don't be afraid to consider some things unworthy of your time. Learn to say "no thanks."

When you are a SL you will be pulled into multiple directions at once. Everyone and every organization will want some of your time. This is the reason why powerful people have executive assistants. An executive assistant's main job is to manage their leader's calendar and to make sure they get to where they need to go on time. Many executives will not only have assistants for their calendar, but also a plethora of other aides in their circle whose main job is to make sure their leader essentially does not need to do anything, but show up. The high level execs do not have time to answer the phones, drop off their laundry, clean the house, or do their own due diligence on hot topics. Many even have drivers. That way there is more time they can utilize doing something else important, rather than drive. Time is the only non-reusable resource.

Time-management is at its most difficult when SLs have to say goodbye. At this point, everyone wants some of your time, so every engagement becomes significant to some degree. Whatever fields you are performing in, you are one of the best. Would you want your favorite of anything to stop? How refreshing is that last cool glass of lemonade on a hot summer day? Or how much better is 15 more minutes of sleep? Like everything else, all things must come to an end. The amount of time you spend doing certain things or at certain places becomes an indicator to others as to who you are. While it may actually have no bearing on you as a person, it becomes the perception to the public. The infamous run into this problem daily. How can an actor, musician, or athlete, ever get any work done or continue on with their life if they always stop to sign an autograph? Even worse, how will a group of your fans feel and perceive you if you have to keep moving and you don't get a chance to shake a hand or sign their memorabilia? As a SL with a tight time schedule, will you stay an extra 20 minutes, wielding your craft to a group? You staying can influence how they look at the world in their eyes or even be the tipping point to the next big thing because you never know what lasting impression you can leave on someone with your words or actions. As a SL, the things you say, show, and do to others will have a far greater impact then you may ever initially imagine. SLs are passionate about what they do. To some high level exec, who is going over their time at an engagement and causing a ripple effect into the rest of their schedule, will at times only stop when their aide (whose primary job is to keep that executive on schedule) abruptly steps in and closes the event. The greatest gift you have to offer will always be your time.

People who value money budget their accounts. You should value your time, more than you do your money. Therefore, budget your time as well. Use your planner and systematically plan your attack. When you budget for time, include how much you spend on: Spiritual growth, family, work, friends, partying, studying, children, etc. Budget it! You have to because as you become a SL, you will realize sooner than later, there is literally not enough time in the day. While budgeting do it for every hour of the day, not just for the day itself. Every decision concerning the use of your time, your talents, and your energies should be measured for efficiency.

Time-management, combined with goal-setting, will change your perception of what you consider "hard." Whatever your measure of difficulty is, it is about to change. It is a consensus among SLs that you can gain knowledge and discipline yourself to perceive a tough job to be easy. People indirectly or subconsciously correlate difficulty with time. Here time, is the indicator of difficulty. This example is used for school. To many, obtaining a master's degree is pretty tough, a primary reason everyone does not have one. To the same people, graduating middle school, is not considered that tough. Well it takes on average three years to graduate middle school and two years to receive a master's degree. Does this make middle school harder than obtaining a master's degree? No. That is how everything in life is. Things are not hard, they take time. If you want to become a rocket scientist, there is a template of time it takes to do that. You must account for the amount of time in school, studying, trial and error, and so forth. If it takes 15 years to become a rocket scientist and you are trying to rush the process and do it in 10, then yes it will seem difficult.

Value your time like you value your money, because in the end you are paying for things with time not with money. One of the most popular thoughts in the average mind when rationalizing a purchase is how much *time* will have to be spent, to earn the money you are about to spend. In a rational mind, that can be the difference between the purchase. When you are arguing with someone, working at a dead-end job, or anything in general that you do, stop and ask yourself—is this worth my time?

70 years. People have grandparents older than the age of 70, but it was a little more than 70 years ago when Adolf Hitler and his regime attempted and almost succeeded in taking over a vast majority of the world. This did not happen centuries ago. People who fought in the war or became victimized are still alive. If negative energy can be expended to do something so tragic and selfish as well as seemingly impossible (take over the world), then positive energy can be applied to becoming a master in a

given domain. It just takes careful planning, persistence, patience, and a little skill. The issue is that many people are too spaced out. Too little energy put in the right things, and too much energy put in the wrong things. Too much time following sports, watching television dramas, or keeping up with the latest events in celebrities lives. Not enough time spent on researching, reading, and pushing yourself to new limits in your field of work.

When you budget your time think about how much you can make in one hour and add up all the hours on things that are a waste of time. Everyone has their vices; everyone needs fun hobbies, and so on, but how many hours do you really need to spend making a fantasy sports team, following every player on and off season, watching all the games, and all the ESPN highlights after. This is not just for sports; it is the same with all hobbies. Sure they are fun, but how much money are you making in these hobbies. Better yet, how much money are you losing with all these uninterrupted hours of diversions? Right now if this makes you angry, if you say hey "I want, and need, these outlets, consistently," then becoming a SL is not for you. Remember these are the small sacrifices you make in the short-term, so you can do what you want forever in the long-term.

During the years of the Cold War between Russia and the United States both countries directed majority of their resources to science and math. The Cold War rivalry between the two nations focused on initial exploration in space, which was seen as necessary for national security and symbolic of technological and ideological superiority. The Space Race had its origins in the missile-based arms race that occurred just after the end of

World War II, when both the Soviet Union and the United States captured advanced German rocket technology and personnel. Both nations had different security strategies for outer space, but they mainly revolved around the application of the missiles. A popular belief was that from outer space you could shoot down a missile, thus making your country almost indestructible from any foreign threat. The Space Race sparked unprecedented increases in spending on education and pure research, which accelerated scientific advancements and led to beneficial spin-off technologies. The United States touched down on the moon and Russia invented a wide array of space programs. This was accomplished in a matter of years.

"Until you value yourself, you won't value your time, until you value your time, you will not do anything with it." -M. Scott Peck-

Chapter 27

DELEGATION

As the SL, become proficient in delegation because people want to work for you and to effectively and efficiently manage your time, you must utilize and incorporate others. Communicate expectations and trust your team to abide by those expectations. No need to reinvent the wheel on delegation. There are two management styles that are widely known and used. Micro-management and macro-management. In the first instance you are the boss, who sometimes may have a perceived low level of trust in your subordinate(s), so you stand over their shoulder as they work, watching and wanting to know every little detail in the process until a jobs completion. In the latter, you are the boss who gives the team a task and trust they use the most 3E way to accomplish it. You cannot do everything, nor should you. It is impossible to become an expert at everything. You may be very good at a variety of things, but not the expert. In the end it is a detriment to you, your brand, and your organization to do it all. People will get frustrated and think you are inept yourself if you don't use them or underwork them. Train and trust those in your organization to hold up their end of the bargain and to get their job done.

It is irrational to think you can do it alone and foolish to believe you do not need your teammates. History illustrates the widespread principle of teamwork throughout centuries. In every military, militia, anything that called a nation to arms (in every part of the world), the shared belief was teamwork. Since the beginning of time people have worked and fought together in teams. It is more effective and efficient, plain and simple. Why attempt to fix a method that is not broke? A SL knows where to place people and how to win with any team they are given.

"In any environment or organization good people prefer activities where they can pursue three things:

Autonomy: People want to have control over their work.

Mastery: People want to get better at what they do.

Purpose: People want to be part of something that is bigger than they are."

Chapter 28

CONTINUING SUCCESS

"Each time you decide to grow again, you realize you are starting at the bottom of another ladder.[1]" Book I spoke about reaching your full potential and since you never reach it stay hungry and stay teachable. You should always be learning and growing. To sustain credibility one must additionally learn to teach themselves. Staying disciplined enough to handle one's affairs and still find time to enter the study will boost you past the competition. SLs recognized the things that got them where they are, may not keep them in the same place. The same reason why an athlete goes broke after their short stint professional careers is the same reason why SLs excel. Once you have become accustomed to a level of pleasure and happiness, you want to either maintain that level or surpass it. In the athletes' case, they are used to spending a certain amount of money to afford themselves luxuries they enjoy. They cannot fathom going backward and losing these privileges and luxuries, so they keep spending past their means. In the SLs case they have also come to expect certain pleasures from exceling in their respected fields and they will not tolerate anything less. This is

---

[1] Ken Rosenthal.

human nature and it is reasonable. So even after you "make it" you must continue to ascend to the next level.

Examine these two situations of two different people on opposing sides of the spectrum. Person A spends their weekend nights on the social scene; clubs, parties, movies, you name it. Person B spends their weekend nights at the library. Who is the person of more interest? Person B is. Surely some character who spends all their time in the library cannot be more interesting than somebody who constantly goes out and experiences new things around the city. Well when you are doing the ordinary it becomes hard for people to respect your mind. No one in leadership positions sees you as a threat and those around you have a limited amount of respect for what you bring to the table intellectually. Essentially the interest others have of you does not lie in you, but in what has happened around you. People will not ask person A how they felt at the party, how they felt about the movie, bar, etc. People ask how the party was, how was the movie, or how was the bar? Essentially you having a good time only matters to your own circle of friends. Now person B is of an interest to everyone. Especially those in superior positions. Why did they not go out on the social scene or stay home and relax? Better yet why did person B go to the library? What are they learning about or doing that is so important they take away their own free time on arguably the two most social nights in the world. Not only will this perplex people, but some of them will not be able to drop this line of questioning until they get the answers they are looking for. Usually there are only two main things the questioning will reveal. That Person B is doing something way out of the lane of the interviewer and they have no interest in pursuing their late night library trips. Or Person B is on to something that can be beneficial to the interviewer as well and they want to know how to get on the bus before it becomes a band wagon. Those in superior positions see this as a threat, those in subordinate positions see this as an opportunity, your peers see it as a partnership, whatever it is, it is interesting. It is a threat to superiors because they now know they must up the ante to ensure you do not catch or overrun them in whatever it is they are already good at. Those subordinates see this as their chance to take it to the next level.

To become relevant or stay relevant in any atmosphere you must continue to grow. If you only go to work when everyone else does then you are not pushing yourself. The "grind" that you always hear of occurs when offices are closed, before the sun comes out, and well after it goes down. When you are tired and ready to give up, but you continue, that is the grind. Working is doing the same things as everyone else at the same time. Working hard is doing a little bit more then everyone in the same time frame. Grinding is working hard and smart, 3E; it is eating lunch when everyone else is starting their breakfast. Even when you reach the top of the path, you will realize there is another one that goes even higher and is even steeper. It is at this moment you will realize you have the tools to reach the peak.

"The day you stop growing is the day you forfeit your potential and it becomes the end of your success."

Chapter 29

THE LITTLE BLUEBERRIES MATTER

In the 1995 hit movie Casino, Robert De Niro plays a Jewish money making mobster, who exemplifies what it means to be detailed. De Niro's character, Sam 'Ace' Rothstein, was no stranger to making plenty of money for his associated crime family. Ace started out as a bookie, but he did so well the "bosses" kept promoting him—if that's even the term in mob culture. Ace was already an infamous bookie. For sporting events it was rumored that he knew everything about every athlete and team; what they did the night prior, if they smoked, even what they ate for breakfast the morning of. Everything. Eventually Ace was sent to Las Vegas, to manage a casino floor, which the mobsters took their cuts off of.

In one scene, while sitting down talking to the general manger of the casino one evening, Ace noticed that the GM's muffin had more blueberries in it, than his own. Ace took both muffins to the chef and told him "that for now on he wanted all the muffins to have an equal amount of blueberries." Ace told the chef he did not care how long it took, but that all muffins will have an equal amount. Spoiler alert, at the end of the movie when the mob bosses were put on trial for their casino dealings, they ordered a [1]"hit" on everyone involved, so no one could testify against them in court. Who out of all the Italian mobsters did they leave alive, Ace, the Jewish bookie. To them, Ace was the bank. Ace was good at what he did and he only kept getting better. Ace had *become irreplaceable.* Now while you certainly won't get a hit taken out against you for not working above expectations, you can get fired or go out of business. This amount of detail is what it takes to be a SL. *All the little things matter,* especially in a world where perception is reality and *someone is always watching.* If you are already in a very high leadership position you should hire people who are this detailed. If you are working to get to an elevated leadership position, you should become this detailed.

Think about the amount of moving parts that go into making your organization 3E. In fact put this same thought into how your career, how your position in life, makes your professional and personal organizations work. If any faction stopped or slowed down somewhere along the continuum, an element of the organization would be at risk. If you stopped working, if you stopped doing your job correctly it can weaken the backbone of the organization and you are only as *strong as your weakest link.* This goes back to taking care of your business with passion. *Every little detail matters.*

---

[1] To kill somebody as part of a financed murder contract.

Here are some highlights of a news article about UPS and their plans of efficiency. What is important to take away is the amount of detail they put into something and the benefit from doing so.

UPS Figures out the 'Right Way' to Save Money, Time and Gas Efficiency is everything for United Parcel Service. Save time, space and money, and get there when promised. But UPS has one low-tech secret to getting deliveries there on time. UPS plots its delivery routes to make as many right turns as possible, trying to avoid turning left. They turn right about 90 percent of the time. Their trucks are also parked just five inches apart with rearview mirrors overlapping.

UPS trucks drove 2.5 billion miles in 2006, but the company says its right-turn routes saved 28,541,472 million miles, three million gallons of fuel, and 1,100 trucks. UPS projected savings of $600 million a year from the changes.
By BRIAN ROONEY
GARDENA, Calif., April 4, 2007 ABC News

"No one rises to low expectations."

Chapter 30

THE MARKET

G ood things come to people who wait, great things come to people who go out and earn it. That is how the saying should go, but these days' good things come to people who go out and earn it and great things go to people who take it. It is one thing to have patience—persevering in the face of delay, it is another to wait. Never wait. Waiting is not ok. Take the word out of your vocabulary. Subconsciously it is rendering you helpless because in the back of your mind someone has told you it was ok to wait. When the president expects something to be done at a certain time, do you think he is ok with waiting? Not only no, but hell no. Waiting is defined as "to remain stationary, to pause, in readiness or expectation." The market today is aggressive, and to succeed you must become assertive in the way you operate. [1]When sharks stop swimming they drown and when you stop producing.., motivating.., operating.., moving.., you share the same fate in the market.

It is a tough economy worldwide, so understanding the market you are in can make or break you. People ascend in the professional world or any realm for that matter once they fully

---

[1] Common Perception.

apply themselves. By continuously applying yourself to your greatest extent, you find safe haven in your work ethic. You know you are not the very best yet, but you also know that with your discipline, adaptability, and the right opportunity you can continue to grow and prosper. You don't worry about being let go of because you know you would be one of the last an organization lets loose—plus you know that you are highly valuable in the marketplace. Continue to PMR, put in your all, and job security is a concern of the past. The "all" includes the due diligence, previously discussed, all the time. Doing the background research, finding new and innovative ways for your company to save more money, make more money, and essentially become more 3E. Figure out answers to morale problems. Become the go to player in your organization for everything. These are all things SLs do and to survive and thrive in the markets today this is who you must transform yourself into. After you become a SL there will be no reason for an organization to ever let you go. Even after you retire, they will want you around for your wisdom. In the worst case scenario, if someone were to let you go, there would be numerous organizations after you.

A perfect example for this is Shaquille O'Neal. Shaq already had an illustrious career up to and through his Lakers years. After the Lakers parted ways with O'Neal, every team was after him. O'Neal had nothing to worry about. O'Neal won another NBA title with the Miami Heat. After a few more years of playing and his body wearing down, Shaquille O'Neal was not the same player he was—physically—when he first started 19 years ago. Still teams outbid each other to have O'Neal on their roster, not solely because of his playing ability, but because of O'Neal's wisdom he could share with younger players, coaches, and the organization alike. O'Neal did play and win with an organization that had been deemed a powerhouse for years, so just the firsthand knowledge he could provide about how people operate to become successful was worth his salary in itself.

A military Public Affairs Officer (PAO) fast tracked his career by becoming known as a person who would get the job done in new, innovative and unheard of ways. During one of this particular PAO posting's, he worked for the Chief of Naval Operations (CNO). This is a very high position in the United States Navy; the CNO is the senior military officer of the Department of the Navy. At the rank of CNO these people are highly qualified and savvy, but they don't always have time to keep up with the minute-to-minute affairs of the public, hence the job of the public affairs officer. The officer acts as an advisor to high ranking military and political figures disseminating information and news up and down the chain of command. During his posting, the CNO was being questioned at a senate hearing. Before the very end of the hearing a recess was call, and it was during this time a senator decided to ask a zinger question to boost his likeability with his constituents and throw off the CNO.

The senator posted a very tough question he was going to ask the CNO on his twitter page. He wanted to get his constituents to tune in for the results and found it amusing. What the senator did not realize is that the public affairs officer had all his bases covered. The PAO had already been following the Facebook pages, tweets, emails, and whatever else he could get his hands on from everyone who could potentially ask the CNO any questions during the hearing. During the recess when the officer caught wind of the twitter question that was going to be directed at his boss, the PAO went to go brief the CNO. The CNO trusting his PAO readied for the question and when the hearing resumed it was answered with such grace and confidence the CNO not only shocked the crowd, but also the senator who was sure he could catch the CNO off guard. When the CNO asked the PAO how he'd figure that random question would be asked the PAO answered with the out of box research he had done.

Now this instance goes out to the whole PAO community, whole chain of command in the Navy, and people in the private/civilian sector catch wind. Just that little bit more work, that ownership of the PAO's job, showed everyone that the PAO could become an expert in the field and this was a career for him. With a continued work ethic and intelligent moves like that his career is not at risk, ever. Someone who goes above and beyond, seeks adverse situations, and figures out innovative ways to solve problems. If you are not doing this at work, in your own business, or in your own personal life, you are wrong. This is the difference between a public affairs officer who may be in limbo of job security, one that is "on track" to their career, and the PAO who eventually made Captain and became a star among his peers. For the people who come to work late, leave early, and don't put forth effort; they may keep the job, but they are less likely to ascend in the organization.

You must become a student of your art. Study past success and failures. If the arena in which you compete in is new, study some of the methods used by others when they created new markets. While the journey to prosperity is tough—it is also full of excitement, new experiences, and fun and you should continuously try to get the most out of it. Here are a few things to remember on your journey to not only get the most out of it, but also to ensure you will not burn out and fall short.

- Work fills a large part of life, so to be truly satisfied do what you love.
  - You will know in your heart when you find out what exactly it is you love. Everything up until then are just experiences you should be happy you have had, at the very least it can help you relate to others. If you are not doing what you love right now, you should still be looking. Keep looking and don't settle for anything less.
- Doing what you love also propels you to do great work.
- Work relationships should be as profound as friends and family.
  - You want to establish intimate relationships. Once you can build the same amount of trust and likeability with your co-worker as you can with a close friend or family member, it will push you to another level in the office.
- Always leave things in a better condition.

- o Your job, team, relationships, leave them all in better shape. Don't be afraid to create or change policy, if you don't then who will? Yes it takes time out of your already busy schedule and yes it is extremely difficult work, but when things are left in better condition you will be revered as a SL.
- People look up to you.
  - o It is selfish for you not to do better, not to have that want—that desire to succeed. You are important, but your lack of desire can cheapen your worth and meaning to the world. It is easy to continue being selfish and to make excuses. Challenge yourself, make it into that private competition. Once you get the hang of it, it will be fun. Once a person understands the game of life, the levels and rules there are, then the world is no longer a trick—it's a game to be played. Master the art of life.

"If you knock at the door of opportunity and
no one answers, break in."

BOOK IV

UNTITLED

This is the book to your life. You name it.

Chapter 31

ACCEPT NOTHING LESS THAN FULL VICTORY

Life lessons can be gathered from studying the classic United States military invasion, D-Day, at the Normandy beaches in France. June 6, 1944, 160,000 Allied troops landed along a 50-mile stretch of heavily-fortified French coastline to fight Nazi Germany on the beaches of Normandy, France. General Dwight D. Eisenhower called the operation a crusade in which "we will accept nothing less than full victory." More than 5,000 ships and 13,000 aircraft supported the D-Day invasion, and by day's end on June 6, the Allies gained a foot hold in Normandy. The D-Day cost was high—more than 9,000 Allied soldiers were killed or wounded, but more than 100,000 soldiers began the march across Europe to defeat Hitler.

United States leadership accounted for many things. They accounted for the exponential number of soldiers who would be lost storming the beach and the overhead air support shot down trying to provide distraction and cover for the ground forces. Soldiers who have lived through the experience have told countless stories about how horrific the invasion was. Some soldiers did not even make it to the beach. Their water craft were either shot down or shot at, so they had to jump out and try to swim the rest of the way to shore. However with all the equipment the soldiers wore, many of them just drowned. Soldiers admitted they were scared, with the water to their back there was no turning around, certain death, but ahead lied a beach crippled with bodies: from explosives, fatal gunshot wounds, or simply just pinned down to one position with nowhere to navigate safely. A beach littered with dead bodies, body parts, and confusion. When soldiers could not go back and had to face a powerful enemy, they dug deeper in their souls and fought more furiously than ever, every second they knew was their last stand as men. If they were to lose they were to go down swinging, biting, clawing, and scratching for every last inch of ground with every last breath. The Allies stormed the beach successfully.

General Eisenhower knew there would be casualties; he also knew while mission success was possible it would not be easily attained. The general did what countless numbers of other military leaders in the past have done; he put his troops in a situation where if they did not go forward, if they did not win, then the only thing certain was death. This is where General Eisenhower's statement he told his troops pre-battle derived from, *"we will accept nothing less than full victory."* In the situation the soldiers were in, that was the only feasible outcome they could accept and fight for, to continue to live on.

What are the consequences if you fail? In your life if you do not accomplish your goals can you still maintain your lifestyle, will you still be able to survive, and will your family for future generations be able to succeed? If not you may need to up the ante, put more eggs in one basket, increase the risk, and the outcome will either be you perishing or your success. In order to excel and become great, you must *put your livelihood at a profound risk*. Life is too short and unpredictable to play it safe. Put yourself in a position of hardship; financial, physical, or just an embarrassing situation, and then flourish. Just from a financial standpoint, you can guarantee this will be the difference between government checks, minimum wage, thousands of dollars, to millions. This is the risk companies bet you won't take and some people simply do not have the courage to take. If you are ready to take that next step, go out on full faith and confidence and excel. Once you do, you will not have any other choice.

"Act like it is impossible to fail."

Chapter 32

BEGINNING OF A NEW CHAPTER

Starting this new journey and rewiring your paradigms are an exciting, but also scary period. Think of how you felt when you went out into the world for your first time. More than likely it was after high school or college. When you literally had to start making perceived decisions for yourself. Some people get so frightened by the thought, they never actually grow up. They stay close and near to what they know. This undoubtedly hinders you in life. The world is so much bigger culturally and geographically, than what you know and by limiting your chances of exploration, you curb your growth. You will get a similar frightened feeling when you begin your new life after reading this guide, but relish in it. Relish on the solitude of the path. Never doubt if you can climb a mountain, instead ask yourself which one should I climb? Attack it and enjoy it, no one can stop you. Watch how much you grow after one year. Just one. The stories and knowledge you will have to pass on to those you meet will put you on a tier you never imagined.

You now know better. You are no longer ignorant or agnostic and the decisions you make from this day forward will be your own. This is the perfect time to pursue whatever it is you want. If you desire to continue to work for other SLs, great.

Large companies are struggling with re-organization, which gives you the perfect opportunity to showcase your aptitude and quickly ascend. Good news is ahead for those willing to take the ultimate risk and strike out on their own. Work labor is cheap, technology is free, and you can now reach a global market online, all things that paint a wonderful picture for small businesses. Either way, when you attempt the impossible, you will always have little competition. Throughout life, stay: flexible, principled, and prepared and many things will work itself out.

Internally you must be replete with bravado and confidence to innovate and enhance—not just things and ideals, but people, cultures, and who you are as well. Where you are going is better than where you have been, even when the path ahead is uncertain.

> "Once you experience an idea or worthwhile concept
> you can never go back. If you immerse yourself in
> it, then there is no force in the world that can take
> it from you…"

King is the CEO of KRBE LLC, a company designed to help others reach elite levels in their craft. He has served as a Naval Public Affairs Officer as a trusted advisor providing intuitive advice to senior level decision makers on a daily basis. During his time in the Navy, he was responsible for developing and presenting briefings for over 500 distinguished visitors, including CEOs, International Media, Congressional Delegations, U.S. and Foreign Ambassadors, and senior military members. His two deployments sparked an insatiable desire to travel, currently visiting or working in over 15 countries and counting. He attended North Carolina State University where he double majored in Political Science and Criminology while earning a scholarship to play football. His list of military awards include four Navy and Marine Corps Achievement Medals, the National Defense Service Medal, Global War on Terrorism Expeditionary Medal, Global War on Terrorism Service Medal, Sea Service Ribbon, Navy Rifle Sharpshooter Ribbon, and the Navy Pistol Sharpshooter Ribbon. After completing SERE school King was asked, "why were you recognized for your outstanding performance while in the Resistance Phase of SERE," he answered, "I honestly don't know."

If you enjoyed this book, then check out my other book on Amazon or www.kingblesss.com:

Capture Your Career: How to Get Any Job or Position You Want in 48 Hours or Less, teaches you the tips, tricks and strategies the nations' top managers use to outshine their peers and realign themselves for professional success.

You can check out my site here: www.kingbless.com
Twitter: @kingblessdotcom
Facebook: @kingblessdotcom
Instagram: @kingblessdotcom

Question? Email me at: king@kingbless.com

Made in the USA
Lexington, KY
20 October 2017